START HERE

YOUR GUIDE TO BUILDING
YOUR MONEY MANAGEMENT SYSTEM

START HERE

MELODY WRIGHT, Ph.D, CFEI

Copyright © 2020 Melody R. Wright

All rights reserved. No part of this book may be reproduced or used in any manner without the prior written permission of the copyright owner, except for the use of brief quotations in a book review.

ISBN: 978-1-7355054-0-4

First paperback edition October 2020.

Edited by Amanda Bert
Cover art by Amber Click

Although the author and publisher have made every effort to ensure that the information in this book was correct at press time, the author and publisher do not assume and hereby disclaim, any liability to any party for any loss, damage, or disruption caused by errors or omissions, whether such errors or omissions result from negligence accident, or any other cause. The information in this book does not replace that of a certified tax professional or that of a certified public accountant.

Just Wright Group, LLC
1754 Woodruff Rd #106
Greenville, SC 29607
www.livebrokeonpurpose.com

This book is dedicated to my Grandmothers, Dorothy Robinson and Beatrice Chapman.

Acknowledgements

I started writing this book at the beginning of 2018. I had such grand plans for it, but before I could even make a dent, life threw new and shiny things in my direction that completely stole my attention away. In 2019 as I was asking God to help me figure out the next steps to take in my business, the Holy Spirit led me to this scripture:

"Now finish the work, so that your eager willingness to do it may be matched by your completion of it, according to your means."
-2 Corinthians 8:11

Now I can proudly say that it is finished.

To God: Thank you for always being in the driver's seat and ordering my steps even when I kicked and screamed the entire way. Your renewing grace strengthens me and your matchless loves reigns supreme. I thank you for this gift that you poured into me to give to others. May you get all the glory from this project and many others you've destined for me to complete.

To my husband, Marcus: You dream so big for me that sometimes it scares me. Thank you for being the yin to my yang, and the peace in my storms. Thank you for loving me and letting me love you. Your support during this project has kept me afloat. I still don't plan on sharing my snacks (wink).

To my dear mother, Rev. Mary Sloan: Hey Girl! Growing up, you always told me, "You'll figure it out" whenever I came to you with a dilemma. I grew to despise that phrase, and I ended up forbidding anyone else from saying these words to me. I now realize that you were preparing me for a life where I would be required to step outside the box to find methods and techniques that would allow me to achieve the dreams and goals that I had. Thank you for being a classic example of a woman who "figures it out." Thank you for covering me with your prayers, your relentless love, and letting me soar.

To my Father, Retired Col. Ronald Robinson: Thank you for your unshakable and generous love. You've let me stumble through life gracefully while always being a firm hand to hold if I needed it. I cherish our Sunday chats and garden talks. My love for processes, procedures, and systems, I got honestly from you.

To my sisters, Dia and Jasmine: I know I get on yall's nerves, but you love me! Thank you for putting up with me, even when Mom told you to ignore me. You've supported my goals and ideas from day one. There's no one else I'd rather have as part of #TeamBunnysKids than you two. Never forget to inquire about "who alls going to be there" when invited to a gathering.

To "Penny": Thank you for believing in this project and for all your generous help along the way.

To Marlena: Girl, you are definitely the salt of the earth and one of the brightest lights on the hill. My sister in Christ. I don't think our meeting was by chance. You've been such a joy to have as a bible study partner, friend and coach. Thank you for all your help with this project.

To the rest of my family and friends that are too numerous to name, thank you for your constant and unwavering support.

Contents

Introduction	1
Transforming Your Money Mindset	8
Nobody Wants to Admit They're Broke	9
Dump The Defaults	13
The Lies We Tell Ourselves	18
Managing Your Money Mindset	22
Under New Management	23
How Do You Feel?	27
So, What's It Gonna Be?	30
What Does Your Financial Success Look Like?	35
Incorporating Your Money Mindset	37
Parental Persuasion	38
Get Into the Game	50
Build Your Money Management System	55
You Don't Always Have to Work Harder	56
A Money Management What?	58
It Starts With Why	63
Mentally Manageable Pieces	66

Demystifying Your Net Worth	70
The Income Station	73
Your Spending Habits Are a Mirror	75
Habits, Trends, and Triggers	77
How Much Should I Be Spending?	80
Cash or Card? Which One Is Best For You?	83
The Budget/Spending Plan Station	87
Your Budget/Spending Plan Is A Box	89
Until There's Nothing Left with Zero-Based Budgeting	93
Trim The Fat	95
The Cost of Cohabitation	98
What If I Don't Make Enough?	100
How To Have a Successful Money Meeting	103
The Savings Station	110
Savings Accounts Save Lives	112
How Much Should I Have In My Emergency Fund?	115
My Emergency Fund Had My Back	119
Where Should I Keep My Money?	123
Stacking Your Non-Retirement Coins	126
In It For The Long Haul	130
Saving When You Don't Have Anything To Save	136
Ready, Set, Save!	139
The Debt Station	141
The Power of $100!	148
Switching Debt Payoff Methods Can Save You Money	150
Not Everyone Wants to be Debt Free and That's Okay	154
Create Your Debt Payoff Plan	156
Manage Your Money Like a Personal Finance Expert	158
Final Words	162
Notes	165

Introduction

"Where do I even start?" This question is one that I asked myself after sitting at the computer, calculating the total amount of debt my husband and I had. The number staring back at me was $212,000. Sadly, I hadn't even added our mortgage yet. So, I asked myself the question again: "Where do I even start?"

You'd think after committing to getting out of debt for the umpteenth time in my life that I'd have a myriad of choices. Yet, I always found myself stuck facing this one solitary question: How do I start? Coming up with those first steps shouldn't have been hard for me. I grew up fascinated by how things worked. I always wanted to know more, and once I mastered that knowledge, I wanted to know even more. Maybe it's why I went all the way down the scientific path to earning my Ph.D. in Microbiology and Immunology with a concentration in Parasitology. I could master the complex life cycle of a malaria parasite; however, mastering my finances always seemed to elude me. Even when I finally found the courage to put one foot in front of the other, I could never seem to keep that stride for long. Something would come along and take me off track. By the time I realized that I'd gotten off track, I'd be so far gone in the comfort of my

START HERE

new situation that getting back on course didn't seem quite as important. That is until the next phase of wanting to get out of debt came around.

How many times have you sat down to conquer your finances and found yourself unable to start? The financial burdens you carry may feel paralyzing. They can leave you feeling trapped in a dark room with no way out. I vividly remember sitting in one of the offices at Wells Fargo, listening to a man explain my loan options to me. What he didn't know was how bad I needed this loan. He didn't know that this personal loan was the only thing I could come up with for trying to cover all of the debt payments we had pouring in. It was my solution to the $212,000 of debt we were faced with paying back. I couldn't ask anyone else for help. He was my only chance. He also didn't know how defeated I felt when he looked up from his computer and told me that the bank was going to send me a letter in the mail with their decision. I knew what that meant; anyone who has ever applied for a loan or credit card knows what that means. It means you've been denied. It means that even though you've been a loyal customer for "X" number of years, those years of loyalty weren't worth taking a chance on you. You could put money into their institution, but they weren't going to be foolish enough to put money back into yours. My debt had become a scarlet letter. No one was willing to help us crawl out of the hole that we'd dug.

When I look back at my life, I can pinpoint an experience that led me to my decision of how I was going to handle my money. This decision resulted in the inability to manage my obsession with spending more money than I had or swiping my credit card with abandon. It was because, at a young age, I told myself that I would never be the one that went without or "didn't have."

When I was younger, we would stay with one of my aunts after school until my mom was able to pick us up on her way home from work. There were a few things I loved about going to her home. One thing that will

INTRODUCTION

always stand out is that we were able to play with my cousin. We would climb trees and play a game called "LumberJack" on an old empty oil heating oil drum in her backyard. And the second thing I loved was the fact that she would sometimes bring us treats home from work. I'm not talking little pieces of candy, either. She would bring us ice cream bars and sometimes even hoagies that we'd split. If there weren't treats, we'd have fruit or other small snacks.

One day while playing outdoors, we all decided to go inside and get a piece of fruit. As I'd been playing with a friend in the neighborhood around my age, I decided that I would bring her an apple, too, so that she wouldn't be left out. As I innocently handed my friend the apple, one of my cousins saw my good deed and ran inside to tattle to my aunt. The way by which my aunt called me into the house immediately alerted me to the amount of trouble that I was in. To this day, I still remember her words loud and clear: "Who told you that you could give that child an apple? Do you think I have enough money to feed the entire neighborhood? Go out there and get that apple back!" My attempt to explain to my aunt that this girl was my friend, and I didn't want her to be the only one not eating an apple only made matters worse. Reluctantly, I trudged outside and asked my friend to give me back the apple. Luckily, she'd only gotten as far as twisting off the stem. As I sulked back into the house to return the apple to the cat calls from my cousins taunting me for getting in trouble, I vowed then and there that I would never not be able to afford to give someone an apple.

That vow I made to myself, along with other experiences where I felt less than compared to the material things other people had, was probably the catalyst for my constant cycle of living beyond my means. You'd think that as a trained scientist that I'd know all about the theory of causation. Yet, I couldn't seem to grasp that the reason for my yo-yo "get out of debt-scapades" was a result of not understanding how to properly manage the

START HERE

money that I had coming in so that I could live the life that I desired. What I could grasp were protocols. Working in the lab, I swore by them. I relied on them so much that I kept them in a 3-ring binder safely inside sleeve protectors. That way, when I was using them during an experiment, they wouldn't accidentally become ruined from a spill, causing me to lose all the precious calculations or notes that I'd collected over the years.

What I needed was a protocol for my money. I needed a set of steps or a guide to show me how to get past the starting point and successfully make my way to the finish line. As a scientist, I learned that introducing the smallest change can result in dramatically positive results. So, that's what I did. Instead of going in cycles and doing the same thing with my finances over and over again, I introduced changes, some big and some small, until I created a protocol like system for my money.

This system is what I like to call my Money Management System. My Money Management System has opened up the door to a level of living within my means that I didn't know was possible. I'm not saying you're going to have to put on a pair of protective eyewear, a white lab coat, and boring closed-toe shoes in the middle of the sweltering summer heat to come up with a plan for how to fix your finances. What I am saying is that getting past the start is going to take you stepping out of your current sequence of attempts and trying something different.

Admittedly, it wasn't easy for this reformed shopaholic to turn her financial life around. But I did, and I'm ready to share how. Some of us have to live those hard lessons so that we can guide others around avoiding them. My journey through my finally-broken debt cycle helped me find my true footing as a faith-based financial coach and certified financial education instructor. I've had a spotlight feature on the Rachael Ray Show, been named one of the "New Money Experts" by Glamour magazine, and worked with several financial institutions to help spread the word on the importance of financial literacy. I wrote this book to address one of the

INTRODUCTION

most consistent comments that I hear from clients and from people I meet at events or through social media: "I don't know how to start." While it may surprise you, not knowing where to start is normal. I should know! Remember, I lived that life.

So, where do you begin? The question itself seems simple, yet when you think about everything that encompasses your personal finances, the answer is not as straightforward as placing your piece on a Monopoly board and rolling the dice when it's your turn. Unfortunately, there is no grand or universal action that marks your beginning. There's no green light or waving of a checkered flag; it's merely you choosing to do something different.

What you may not recognize is that you've already done that. You are doing something different right now. Realizing that something had to change with the way you handled money signifies your beginning. Reading this book signifies your beginning. Every time you make an attempt to change, you're designating your starting point. I wish every time someone decided to get serious about their finances, confetti would fall, and a personal cheering squad would magically appear, but that's not reality. I don't want you to take this moment lightly. It should be celebrated! Do you know how many people don't even make it to this point? I am thrilled to start this journey with you.

You should also know that the beginning can be lonely. You are making a decision to be selfish. You're choosing to put your future and your family's future ahead of anything else. You're closing doors on things that have been a part of you, sometimes for your entire life. That can be hard, which is why I'm here to support you along the way.

In addition to giving you a place to start, I also wrote this book because I want you to experience what it means to live a life where you have options. I don't want you to continue singing those same sad songs about your money or refusing to talk about your finances at all. Instead, I

START HERE

want to give you the tools to create the life that you've been daydreaming about. In the "Transforming Your Money Mindset" section of this book, I'm going to show you how to move from the fear, anxiety, and uncertainty of not knowing where to start to a new level of handling your money. You will receive guidance on moving past default behaviors and understanding how your past impacts your present. You will be empowered to speak the financial freedom you want into existence and change your mindset in such a way that you put your finances under new management. In the "Build Your Money Management System" section, you will learn how to build your own Money Management System using the blueprint that I am going to provide for you. I will break down each piece of the system and show you how to finetune it to best meet your needs. This is the same Money Management System that has helped me and my family pay off over $100,000 of debt and save six months' worth of living expenses. Because of this system, we give more, invest more, and live a life where the stress of money no longer invades our thoughts. It is the same Money Management System that I teach to coaching clients and in classes. It is also the foundation for which I share financial literacy education with the fans and followers on various social media platforms. It helps you identify the causes of your spending, put a spending and savings plan in place, and choose the best method for paying off your debt. This book will help you discover what's been holding you back from stepping in line with the things that you desire to achieve, using the provision that has been gifted to you.

This book is different from other personal finance books in that I'm not giving you a one-size-fits-all method. Doing so would be me denying the fact that we are all created differently. What I am doing is teaching you how to visualize your finances as a whole and how to use the system to develop a plan that works best for you. Through my experiences and the shared stories from clients, I am showing you how your money and your

INTRODUCTION

actions work together. From that connectivity, you can either create the life that you desire or continue to live in your current state.

Challenge yourself to push to the end of this book. Build a Money Management System for yourself. The work is worth it. I want you to be able to say the same things others have said, such as:

- This system took my finances that I felt like was one big jigsaw puzzle with over 1000 pieces and turned it into three pieces that fit seamlessly together.
- I would never have been able to visualize my finances working together like this.
- This is the financial structure and organization that my family needed for us to reach our goals, and you made it seem so easy!

You may even find yourself saying, "I already checked off several items on my financial roadmap, and all I did was build the system!" Remember what I said about small changes—they start now. It begins with you ceasing to tell yourself that your situation is too bad, or that you'll never be able to make a change. It starts with you believing that maybe, just maybe, you can master this money thing after all. Because you can!

Moving forward, consider me your unofficial accountability partner. To kick things off, I want to ask you a huge favor. I want you to email me (StartHere@livebrokeonpurpose.com) and let me know you're starting! Seriously, I want to celebrate this milestone with you. Because I make it a point to answer all of my emails, you can rest assured that you're going to be speaking directly with me. So, let's get this party started!

TRANSFORMING YOUR MONEY MINDSET

Nobody Wants to Admit They're Broke

We were one emergency away from bankruptcy. That's how bad things were. My entire mindset shifted the moment I saw our total debt and realized I had no clue how we could dig our way out. We had a home, we had cars, we had nice clothes and designer things, but we were also one life event away from having the rug pulled completely out from under us. That's hard to know and hard to admit.

Acknowledging that you're broke for many people is akin to admitting defeat. In this day and age, we have a tendency to share every intricate part of our lives. Of course, no one wants to reveal that their life is all smoke and mirrors. But admissions are powerful.

Have you ever stopped to think about why one of the first steps in substance abuse meetings is for meeting goers to admit their problem? They don't do it as a way to bond or fit in. Personal admittance of a problem is a superhuman way to reject the idea that they are powerless and their problem is unmanageable. It levels the playing field, and invites each person to step up and take charge. Similarly to those meeting attendees, you must acknowledge and come face-to-face with the things plaguing

START HERE

you and your finances the most. Many will never make it past this step. Admitting that there is a problem triggers an explosion of other thoughts that can cripple your present beliefs. You want to be happy, you want to change, but for some reason, you won't give yourself permission to do so.

Experts call this "psychological rigidity," a defense mechanism one invokes to protect against those feelings of imperfection, inadequacy, and weakness. Instead of admitting that there is a problem, they look for other ways to justify their behavior. There's a line in one of my favorite Kirk Franklin songs that goes "...but if I keep on doing the things/ that keep on bringing me pain/ there's no one else I can blame/ if I'm not happy." I'd heard this song several times, but I always glossed over the lyrics. Then, one day while driving to work, I actually paused all the noise going on in my head to listen to what the song was saying: "If you're tired of being the same/ if you're tired of things not changing/ it's time for you to get out the way." Kirk Franklin is right. We hold the power to our happiness in our hands. If we want it, we have to take it even if it means admitting there is a problem, changing habits, or removing ourselves from toxic situations. Change happens when we get out of our own way.

Our thoughts can be a scary place. They can hold us hostage and force us to believe things that are untrue. Nobody wants to admit that they're broke, just like no one wants to admit to themselves that they ate an entire carton of ice cream in one sitting while binge-watching an entire Netflix series. What would people think if they knew that about you? What would you think about yourself? Admittance forces us to come face to face with the issues that we continually sweep under the rug. Admittance forces us to face what we believe to be our failures.

What if I told you that your failures offer an exclusive set of information that you would not be able to access otherwise? Think of your failures as those small little lights along a walking trail to help guide your way. When you admit you've made a mistake, developed a bad habit, or don't understand how to do something, give yourself permission to ask

NOBODY WANTS TO ADMIT THEY'RE BROKE

why.

"Why?"

Do you know how loaded that three-letter word is? If not, watch an inquisitive toddler in action. The question "why?" allows you to dig deep into that perceived failure and look for the path lights that will lead you to success. If you don't want to admit that you're broke, but all the signs are pointing in that direction, ask yourself why. This question doesn't have to be accusatory or said with indignation. Instead, imagine this scenario:

You have a quiet moment to yourself. Maybe you are thinking about bills that need to be paid or a purchase you wish you could make... Then, you say, "I don't want to admit that I'm broke or have trouble managing my money."

Unexpectedly, an inquisitive toddler asks, "Why?"

Letting this exchange play out and then thinking through your answer can help start the self-reflection process.

If you're struggling to find the courage and the confidence to address your financial issues, take some time, and answer the following questions.

- Why is it so important for you to stay exactly where you are in your life?
- What will admitting that you're not the best at managing your money do?
- What will this admittance change about your present situation?
- What feelings will it unleash?

Once you've completed these questions, take time to reflect on them. Your current situation, habits, and feelings don't have to be where you stay. Give yourself permission to use your perceived failures and the information they provide as a launching pad to move forward. Those path

START HERE

lights that you uncover will tell you what your money habits are. They will shed light on your default behaviors and mindset. They will tell you what money concepts make you nervous or excite you. They will show you what you're good at and reveal the areas where you need a little more improvement. Admitting you're broke isn't about belittling yourself. It's promising yourself that things will go up from here.

Dump The Defaults

Our thoughts surrounding money don't form overnight. As we start to see how money works in our daily lives, our understanding of money forms. When our awareness of how people use money grows, money habits take shape. This starts so much earlier in life than we often realize.

In our household growing up, a lot of things about money were taught, and a lot of things were not. This lack of purposeful and consistent financial literacy was not due to my family's unwillingness to show me wrong from right. Instead, some of the omissions or misguidances came from the fact that they simply did not know the information themselves. Nonetheless, both the money moves I saw and the ones I didn't see laid the foundation for my default money behaviors.

Default behaviors are our typical, automatic responses and actions. Think about what happens when you reset an electronic device. It goes back to its basic factory settings. Any special programming, improvements, or shortcuts that you installed have been wiped clean, and now the device goes back to functioning the way it would as if you just pulled it out of the box. Basically, it goes back to what it knows to do. As humans, when we are faced with challenges, lack of interest, or fear, we revert to our default behaviors. Why? It's a retreat. In our minds, we've labeled those default behaviors as being "safe."

In the book *Your Default Settings: Adjust your Autopilot to Build a More Stable and Impactful Life*[1], Rad Wendzich calls these repeated behaviors and beliefs "default settings." He describes the development of these settings as stemming from things we do every day. We also discover them by comparing ourselves to others. Think about the patterns, actions, and words that make up a large part of your everyday life. Our sayings, our interactions with others, and even our eating habits all make up our default behaviors. Unbeknownst to us, our default behaviors or settings are mostly shaped by our environment. We form our behaviors based on the behaviors of others. You may find that everyone in your family washes the dishes a certain way. In other households, their way of dishwashing could cause you to clutch your proverbial pearls. My default behavior when it comes to washing the dishes is to not leave them soaking in the sink. My co-workers quickly realized that this was one of my biggest office pet peeves when it came to the break room. Knowing our own default behaviors can help guide our interactions with others. They can also help us understand ourselves better.

Our present behaviors are a representation of our past experiences. I have a strong dislike for dishes being left in the sink to "soak" because my parents never allowed it when I was growing up. We had to use elbow grease. So now, no matter what anyone says about how you should wash dishes, this is the method that I want to revert back to. My mind tells me it's right and safe. If you pay attention, you'll find lots of things that you default back to because of your past. Some are good, and some are bad. As much as you might want to, you can't change the past. You can, however, learn from it, and use that knowledge to change your defaults to behaviors and habits to give yourself a positive advantage.

DUMP THE DEFAULTS

Certainly, there have been times when you watched a member of your family in action and said to yourself, "That's where I get that from!" The conscious and unconscious internalized behaviors surrounding money are tied closely to the people we were surrounded by growing up. These patterns shape our default behaviors.

Take a moment to reflect and ask yourself these questions:
1. How do your finances now differ from that of your parents growing up?
2. How do they differ from that of your parents now?
3. Do you find yourself repeating the same destructive behaviors or have you been able to pull away from the habits you saw holding them back?

In becoming a Financial Empowerment Coach, I've had several discussions with clients surrounding things not taught to us growing up. These conversations are essential. They can help us understand the *why* behind some of our actions our default money behaviors. Yet, it is important not to overlook what you *were* taught through the words and actions of others. Many of the lessons I gleaned about money came from watching my mom, grandmothers, aunts, and uncles interact with their money. It's through them that I learned how to correctly use the word "broke" in a sentence concerning my finances. They taught me how to stretch a dollar and how to make ends meet when it looked like there was more month left than there was money available. I learned how to bargain hunt, how to write a check, and how to float one. I also learned why I should always carry cash in my wallet just in case. While these lessons may not have been the most beneficial in the long run, they were necessary for the time and era in which I was growing up—a period when most people were just trying to make it.

START HERE

Before you read this and side-eye my family, please know that lifelong useful financial lessons were indeed incorporated in my upbringing. As a matter of fact, I still have the same bank account that my mother took me to open with Wachovia—which became Wells Fargo—when I was in high school. I can still vividly remember my mom telling me I wasn't ready for a credit card when I was excited about getting an offer in the mail.

I'd acquired my own set of default behaviors from my family's life lessons surrounding money, but there were still some key details I didn't know. Those gaps in understanding seem to be what most people want to focus on when it comes to their own childhood. The reason why so many of us only focus on the things not taught is that we're looking to place blame on anybody but ourselves for our shortcomings. We already have to take responsibility for so much in our lives, so why should we have to take responsibility for things that other people didn't teach or tell us? The reason why is because taking responsibility is a form of empowerment. Regardless of what you learned or didn't learn growing up, we all have choices to make today.

Can you now see why the first step in AA is so significant? It's about you accepting the decisions you've made and committing to the processes and actions that will help you correct them. This is you resetting your default behaviors of shifting blame or looking for a "get out quick" excuse. From here on out, let's avoid using the phrases "I wasn't taught" or "I never learned" as default statements. These types of responses emphasize words when it's really time to focus on actions. Let's flip these phrases we've grown so comfortable with defaulting to and turn them into change-inspiring affirmations. Instead of saying "I wasn't taught" or "I never learned," turn your default statement into one that takes responsibility and encourages deliberate action.

For example, try these phrases as replacements:

- *"I never learned how to budget, but I'm committed to doing more research and seeing which methods work best for me."*
- *"The importance of saving and investing wasn't taught in my household, but I know how vital these things are for building wealth. Consequently, I'll speak with a financial advisor on how I can get started.*

Do you see how this new phrasing instantly changes the narrative? You're not allowing yourself to fall into your normal default position of complacency. It takes you from being the victim to the victor! It not only inspires a shift in you, but it inspires a difference in those around you. Imagine if you and a group of friends always got together to lament your finances, and you showed up with a whole new outlook, excited for a change. The climate of the group would shift. Action breeds more action. It's contagious, and we all know that to see a difference in life, we have to *be* the difference.

The Lies We Tell Ourselves

Have you ever stopped to think why manifestation rituals are becoming increasingly popular? Practitioners believe that if they think about what they want hard enough and keep their actions in line with that thinking, then whatever it is will come to fruition. There's truth to this. The words that we think and speak have the power to shape our reality.

Because of this, the way we think and speak about our finances is very important. If nothing else, limiting self-talk is a self-fulfilling prophecy. The idea of having a scarcity mindset comes from believing that you don't have the ability to create a better future—or maybe that you simply aren't deserving of one. A scarcity mindset also keeps us from adapting to change. It causes us to be jealous of those around us who have been able to make life shifts that we desire and to only focus on our shortcomings. A scarcity mindset is tied to lack, and lack is tied to the poverty of being without. With this form of thinking, we've defeated ourselves before even getting to the starting line, without even sizing up the competition.

Here are a few of the lies we tell ourselves:
1. 1. I've been struggling with money for most of my life, and I'm

fine. There's no point in changing things now.
2. I don't make enough money to do anything significant with my finances.
3. There will always be a debt that I'll have to pay.
4. My student loans are "good" debt, and I'll be able to pay them off once I get a job in my field.
5. The only way people can pay off a lot of debt is because they don't have children.
6. The only way I can get ahead is if I make more money.
7. I'm not good with money.
8. Budgets are restrictive, and I work too hard to be told what to do with my money.
9. There's no need to save because I can use my credit card to bail me out.
10. If I can increase my credit score, everything will get better.

These lies aren't just simple white lies that we can walk away from. They become ingrained into our being. When you always tell yourself that you aren't enough or you'll never have enough, you begin to live out those lies each day. We live in a world where we are lied to every single day. Why add yourself in the cacophony of those doing the lying?

It's time to flip the script and end the negative self-talk. Separate yourself from the lies. No matter what you believe at this moment, I can promise you this: You were designed for greatness. No one was placed here just to be mediocre. Mediocrity is for those who just want to skate by in life. You, Friend, were meant to soar!

Think back to that time when you just did something so magnificent that you couldn't help but acknowledge it and give yourself a pat on the back. Maybe your recipe was a hit at the get-together, you nailed an

START HERE

important presentation, or you finally found the nerve to try out a new hairstyle or a new makeup technique that made you look amazing. What great compliments did you give yourself? How did that moment make you feel? Come on, don't play coy—we've all hyped ourselves up at some point. There are many days I look in the mirror and proudly tell myself how excellent I am for something others would perceive to be minuscule. Do you know why I do this? It's because, in life, you have to be your own biggest cheerleader. If you aren't rooting for yourself constantly, you can't expect others to pick up that slack. So think back to that feeling you had at that moment. Channel it. That is the same attitude I want you to have with your finances moving forward.

Flipping your finances is a big deal, but I know you aren't reading through this book because you're bored. You want to change your life! Change can happen instantaneously once we make up our minds. It's really that simple. Think back to an interview you recently watched where someone was asked about something life-changing they had recently done. The common theme you'll find amongst all interviewees is that each person simply made a decision. Whether it was to lose weight, take a class, start a business, interview for a job, or something else. They made the decision to do something, and then they did it! Instead of sitting in their current state, they changed their minds and decided they wanted something different.

When you choose to think about your life from a position of abundance or a place of victory, you subconsciously begin to manifest positive change into your life. When you think about having more, you can do more, even if the starting materials are the same. How you approach it from a place of abundance will be different from how you would have approached it from a place of scarcity.

Start today by speaking this abundance into existence with positive affirmations:

THE LIES WE TELL OURSELVES

I affirm that…
- Everything attached to me wins.
- I have ENOUGH.
- I am a Money Magnet. My bills are paid, and I have excess in my accounts. We want for nothing.
- My children's children will reap the benefits of my positive financial habits.
- I am rich in all things. God favors me and rewards me for my obedience to his word. My cup runneth over.

Take some time and write out financial affirmations that you feel will help you during this financial journey. Put them in conspicuous places where you'll be able to seem them as you go about your day to day task. Whenever you start to feel the smallest inkling of doubt or discouragement, refer back to these affirmations and use them to help instill positive feelings towards your situation and your finances.

MANAGING YOUR MONEY MINDSET

Under New Management

For those of us who have had the luxury of traveling by plane, you may recall hearing the flight attendant give instructions to passengers, saying, "In the case of an emergency, secure your own oxygen mask before assisting others." Some people may find this act to be incredibly selfish. How can you, in good conscience, put on your face mask first when there is possibly a small child, an elder, or a person with a disability next to you who needs assistance with their mask? The urge to help others in times of crisis is entirely natural. In all honesty, if you didn't, society wouldn't let you live it down. However, there is a logical reason why the flight attendants give this particular set of instructions.

How can you help someone else if you haven't helped yourself first?

Think about it. In the event of an emergency where God forbid, you need to use your oxygen mask; you won't be able to help anyone if you can't breathe. This same logic applies to your finances. We all want to be in a position to help family and friends. In some cultures, it's standard practice that the children take care of the parents once they've reached a certain level of financial success. This happens regardless of their parents' financial standing. First-generation college graduates and those in the family who've gone on to be more successful than other family members usually feel the weight of this unspoken responsibility more.

While generosity and acts of kindness are something we all should strive to incorporate into our lives, it can also be a significant deterrent for getting out of a financial rut. I've spoken with many clients who find themselves living paycheck to paycheck and without adequate savings. Why? After making sure everyone else is okay, there isn't anything left for themselves.

I've also witnessed this firsthand with my husband, who is a natural giver. We were at his family reunion years ago, and everyone was packing to leave. While sitting in my car waiting for him to finish his goodbyes with his family, I noticed that he was handing out wads of money to people. Of course, this piqued my interest. As his girlfriend at the time, I was wondering where my bundle of money was. When he got back to the car, I casually asked him why he was giving so many people money. He explained that he just wanted to help them out with paying for gas to get back to their locations.

I didn't push the issue back then. (Just so you know, he didn't give me any gas money so that I could get back to my location, which I do still bring up every now and again.) After we were married, he confessed to me that he'd subconsciously taken on the role of the "responsible" one. Because he made it, he had to make sure others were okay, too, even if it was a detriment to himself.

These unspoken expectations and self-imposed rules can feel paramount. But there's another towering reality to consider. Simply put, you can't water others if your well is empty. Whether or not you feel it's a moral obligation or you want to be in a position to bless others, you will never be able to create financial sustainability for yourself if you don't put yourself first at some point. Putting yourself first is easier said than done, especially when family members have come to rely on you as a source of income. There may be some who have a legitimate need, while there are others who will see you as a bottomless ATM. To build your own financial stability, you're going to need to incorporate boundaries around your finances.

I am a huge fan of boundaries and let others tell it. I just don't have boundaries; I have moats with alligators around certain things in my life. Boundaries aren't only effective for keeping things out or protecting your peace. They can also positively limit your room of operation. You don't have to stop helping people cold-turkey; you can start by putting boundaries around how much you want to give by including this as a line item in your budget or spending plan. (We'll talk more about budgets and spending plans later in the Money Management System section of this book.) By deciding how much money you want to give, you're doing two things. You're placing boundaries around the rest of your money, and you're confronting the reality of your finances. When you have a finite amount of resources to work with, you quickly realize that not everyone can have access.

There are those who won't be happy to know that the First National Bank of YOU is now closed or has limited hours. Some might feel resentful. Others may bring up how many times they did things for you as you were growing up to guilt you into feeling obligated to help. Most won't or don't want to understand your reasons for saying "no" or "I don't have it." In their eyes, you've been cast as the villain instead of the hero. That's hard, but it's also OK. In fact, it's necessary.

We see this scenario play out far too often in the lives of athletes and celebrities. They're rich and famous one moment and famously broke the next. The only way we can all make it is if we give others the room to set

START HERE

up financial legacy pillars for the next generation that comes behind us. You can't save money to purchase a home if you're continually paying the bills of those who don't want to live within their means. You can't invest or start a business if you're continually loaning money that you'll never see again. You only owe people your love, your respect, and your best. You do not owe them all of your money.

How Do You Feel?

If there was an award for the topic of discussion that drummed up the most feelings, you could bet anything that finances would be in the running. My emotions surrounding finances have run the gamut from utter despair to absolute exhilaration. In some ways, it can feel like a never-ending roller coaster ride. One minute you're at the top, living your best life (or lie). Then, in what can feel like the blink of an eye, you find yourself at the bottom, covered in debt and incoming bills. We often wear a mask to hide the turmoil we feel inside from the outside world. At the same time, we also use that mask to try and disguise the situation from ourselves.

When was the last time you had a "come to Jesus moment" with yourself about your money? When was the last time you looked in the mirror and admitted to yourself how *your* actions contributed to *your* dilemma? Have you permitted yourself to get angry or to actually have a good cry concerning your money? If not, I want you to stop reading this right now and do just that. Because I know you're still reading, I want you to stop bottling up every emotion you have concerning your finances and

START HERE

just let it go! Take off the mask, stop being the strong one, stop being the bank, stop being everything to everybody, and be what you need to be the most with yourself:

Truthful.

At some point in your life, someone probably told you, "get out of your feelings," but now I want you to do the exact opposite. I want you to get into them. How you're feeling at this moment is going to be markedly different from where you will be three months from now.

As you begin to make behavioral changes surrounding your money, you may feel like what's asked of you is too much. Of course, this reaction is understandable. We're not only shifting your mindset, but we're also shifting your actions and responses in the form of altering habits. It is easy to trick yourself into thinking your old habits are more comfortable when faced with the task of tackling a substantial debt. Remember, being too comfortable is what got you into this mess in the first place.

Moving forward, I want you to start a money journal. By writing down the rawest of your emotions in the journal, you can refer back to them when you feel like the journey is becoming too hard. Use it as a comparison for how you're feeling at that moment. It can also be used to identify the areas in your life that have become better since you took action. You'll be able to admit to yourself that even those things that feel hard aren't as bad as they used to be. Things that are easy to you now never started out being easy. Trust me, each day you choose to show up for yourself and purposely take control of your finances, you'll find your situation is 1% better than the day before.

The small changes aren't always noticeable when we are in progress, but perfection is in the doing. During my first attempt at fixing my finances, I kept a money journal. In it, I wrote down all my feelings surrounding

HOW DO YOU FEEL?

money, any new money tips I learned, my plan for getting out of debt, our amortization schedules, the stocks I wanted to purchase, and how much I would bring in each night waiting tables at my part-time job. One day while cleaning, I found it tucked away in a box with some other old books. As I leafed through the pages, I was taken on a journey back in time to when I first realized that I had to make a financial change. As I read through each page, I saw the growth that I experienced and the lessons I learned. Even though I ended up making some financial mistakes again due to changes in life and other things having priority above my finances, finding the journal was a reminder that if I did it before, I could do it again. This time, those lessons were going to stick!

So, What's It Gonna Be?

Several years ago, Marcus and I sat in the living room of our newly purchased home that we couldn't really afford watching late-night TV. As new homeowners, we enjoyed watching shows on HGTV and the DIY Channel. Every now and again, we'd find ourselves watching the financial guru Suze Orman on CNBC.

This particular night as we were watching the Suze Orman Money Class, I couldn't help but become entranced by her message. She was speaking of life without debt. She made it all sound so easy. All you had to do was talk about it and then work towards paying it off! Who couldn't follow those easy steps?

Me, I couldn't. As I sat entranced by her message of debt freedom, I was also paralyzed with fear. I knew that for me to move forward, it would mean being open and honest with myself and with my husband. Even though I longed for life without debt, I was too afraid to open my mouth. So I sat and watched the rest of the show in silence.

Have you ever been afraid just to start? To really start, you have to cut out all the noise and dive into whatever it is your soul is pushing you to do at the time. Maybe it's taking a class to learn a new skill, applying for a job that you don't necessarily feel qualified for, or even respectfully sliding into the DMs of that cutie who keeps popping into your Twitter feed. Anytime we're being pushed in a positive direction, you can count on a contrary feeling forcing its way into our lives in the form of self-doubt, hesitation, and fear.

So what's truly holding you back from pursuing what you deserve in life? Only you can answer that question. For me, when it came to getting out of debt, it was the fear of people thinking I was a fraud or a failure that held me back. Debt, to me, also meant defeat.

Debt said that I wasn't smart enough to handle my finances, and I recklessly let things get out of control to the point where I was silently screaming for someone to save me. While sitting there watching that Suze Orman Money Class, my mind kept wondering what Marcus would think. How would he react if I told him the current total of my student loans? Would he yell? Would he no longer trust me to handle our finances? Would he want a divorce? I allowed those fears to take over, and I stayed silent for another two years before I finally had enough.

There is a difference between being broke and living Broke on Purpose. No one chooses to *be* broke, but many times, they can choose whether or not they *stay* that way. Growing up, the word "broke" was always thrown around our household. It was used in the context of not having any money. Like every child, I picked up the term and started applying it to my situation when my cash was looking a bit funny. If my account didn't hold the amount of money that I deemed good enough for my situation, I was "broke." If I couldn't afford to go out with my friends, I would reply, "Girl, I'm broke." The difference between my past and that current Broke On Purpose situation is that in the past, I wasn't broke because I wanted to be, I was broke because I allowed my choices to make me that way.

You may find that people don't like to use the word "broke." For many people, it has an understandably negative connotation. It implies that you don't view yourself as being whole or complete. It gives the impression that something is irrevocably wrong in your life. In the beginning, we weren't just broke. We were Aimlessly Broke. Think about the word "aimlessly" for a second. It means *without purpose or direction.* That is a spot-on description of what our finances looked like at the time. We didn't have a solid financial plan. We didn't have any savings to speak of, and we sure as heck didn't have a direction for our family. Sure, we had goals: We wanted to buy a better house and to be able to travel more. However, what it ultimately boiled down to was that we'd gotten too comfortable living a basic life—this feeling of being comfortable trumped any commitment to make a change.

After those two years of silently wanting to make a financial change, our situation finally forced me to stop hiding in the shadows and step up to the plate. I was ready to be Broke on Purpose. When you think of the phrase Broke On Purpose® means just what it implies. I decided to be broke instead of allowing someone or something else to choose that way of life for me. What if, instead of allowing that word to have power over you, you claimed control over it? That's just what I did when I unashamedly proclaimed myself to be "broke." I decided that I would no longer be held captive by my finances. If I was going to be broke, instead of setting myself up for financial failure, I was going to set myself up for financial success. There would be no penny spared in the process. I was going to live as if I was monetarily broke, but on purpose!

Switching to living Broke on Purpose didn't immediately happen overnight. Of course, there was a mindset and habit shift, but I also had to look at what those path lights were revealing to me about my past behavior. Our past holds valuable lessons. Believe it or not, many of these lessons are put into our lives purposely to prepare us for the next big thing coming (it would be great if we knew that beforehand huh?).

SO, WHAT'S IT GONNA BE?

I wish I could tell you that I was always excited and committed to our finances. I wish I could tell you that it didn't take me realizing we had $212,000 of debt for me to shake myself out of the fog. My husband and I sometimes sit around and talk about what we'd do if we could go back in time to change things. Reminiscing on the past can be fun, but it can also be dangerous, causing you to invite feelings of self-doubt, frustration, and anger into your life. When I noticed that these conversations would always leave me in a loathsome mood, I'd have to do some digging to look for the silver lining in it all. I'd have to look at my path lights. What were the lessons I was supposed to learn? Even in all of this financial chaos and turmoil, there were indeed lessons being taught. Because we made so many mistakes with our finances in the past, we are now able to use those mistakes as guides for the future. We experienced what happened when we lived beyond our means. Now, we can commit to not making that mistake again.

One of the biggest lessons I learned was that I had to stop being so inattentive to our monthly cash flow. For instance, I've always been the one to do the budget in our household. If we're keeping it real, most women are. Some months were better than others, but my husband and I have always strived to live what we considered to be a comfortable life. Now, comfortable is relative. For me, being comfortable meant I typically didn't allow myself to go without something if there were a reason to have it. We weren't going crazy buying flashy things, but we didn't deny ourselves nice dinners or new outfits every now and then. It didn't seem like we were living beyond our means, but we definitely were.

The budgeting system that I used was an Excel spreadsheet. I'd create the budget at the beginning of the month, and every Sunday, I would sit down and reconcile the budget based on what we'd spent that week. At least, that was my intention. I didn't keep up with it as well as I should have. There were some months where I wouldn't reconcile until the end of the month, completely missing the signs that we were overspending in specific areas long before the month ended.

We lived this life for years. Sometimes the bug would hit me, and I'd say, "Hey, we might need to focus on paying off some of this debt!" But that feeling would wear off pretty quickly, and we'd be back to our old ways. Does this sound familiar? It's the story many people live.

The lesson that I learned here was that in order for our finances to stay consistently on track, it meant we had to consistently budget. No checking in when we felt like it. None of those occasional "Hey big head!" or "What you doing?" texts. We had to be laser-focused on the plans we had for our money and where our money was actually going.

So, you have a choice to make. Either you want that change you've been dreaming about, or you're content with staying the same. This time, I want you to think about what's at stake. Write it down in your journal, pray on it, meditate, or do whatever you need to do. But, here is where you decided if you push past whatever may be holding you back. Here is where you decide if you're going to start.

What Does Your Financial Success Look Like?

Have you ever heard the saying, "You can't see the forest for the trees"? That's what living in a state of financial overwhelm can do to you. It creates this unyielding need to focus solely on the issues at hand while denying yourselves the beauty of the future. All you are able to see is the tree right in front of your feet rather than the entire trail throughout the forest, stretching across a bright horizon.

How can you think about what life looks like on the other side of debt when you're too busy trying to keep yourself from drowning in it? I remember trying to get started. I went from bank to bank trying to get a loan to consolidate all of my debt so that my payments would be more manageable. No matter how many banks I visited, no one would help. Even though I'd been with those banking institutions for years, my debt was a stain that they didn't want to touch. It was as if I was wearing a scarlet letter.

Here's the thing: We've all been told "No" in response to something that we truly needed. Every time those banks told me no, it would make me doubt if this whole getting-out-of-debt thing was even possible. I wondered if I'd dug us a hole so deep that there was no way out. That was my scarcity mindset in full action. Remember scarcity equals lack, and lack equals poverty. Because I believe in the power of our words, I knew I had to flip the script I was using to speak to myself. I started to talk to myself differently about our situation. I accepted that the banks were turning down my request for loans to consolidate our debt. That didn't mean it was the only option available to me.

Even at the lowest points, I knew I could experience life at a higher magnitude than what I was allowing myself. The way to get past the rejections that I was receiving was to keep the scenarios, where I told myself "Yes!" at the forefront of my mind. I wrote the vision. In these visions, I detailed the way I wanted our lives to look.

You have to ask yourself, "What version of yourself do you *want* to be?" Do you want to feel as if you're never going to have enough money for the rest of your life, or do you want to get to a point where you're able to be the lending hand? By changing my way of speaking and thinking, I gained the upper hand. I battled the negative using the positive, and I spoke life into the things that only existed in my dreams. When I had conversations with my husband (or heck, anyone who would listen!) about our finances, I would always talk about plans for the future. I knew if I continued to focus on what our life looked like after debt, then my actions in the present would follow suit to help get us there.

I've mentioned your dreams and goals a lot. In those dreams, I'm sure you've thought about financial success. So what does it look like to you? Don't look at someone else's paper for the answer to this question. There is no cheat code. Only you know what success looks like to you. For me, it meant I was able to breathe and that I didn't have the burden of unnecessary debt. It meant that we had room to do more with our money than just pay bills. Success isn't a one-dimensional thing. So, what does financial success look like to you?

INCORPORATING YOUR MONEY MINDSET

Parental Persuasion

I remember having a conversation with a young lady about her burning desire to purchase a home within the calendar year. She was still working on her finances, and due to a lot of hard work, things were falling into place. When I inquired as to why she had to buy a home that particular year instead of waiting until she felt fully ready, she gave her daughter as her reason. Specifically, her daughter was getting older, and she wanted to give her the chance to live in a home before she left for college. She elaborated, saying how important it was to her because it was something she wasn't able to experience when she was a child. To dive deeper, I inquired how owning a house made it more of a home than what she was able to provide now. She responded that it didn't. She was still able to give her daughter a loving home despite not owning the house itself. Her desire to buy a home at this particular point was in response to other's opinions that were making her feel that her financial journey and choices were invalid. She was intent on purchasing a home simply because she saw others around her purchasing a home. The deafening noise from the societal pressures that each of us face every day made her feel that her best wasn't good enough.

We all have a natural inclination to want to give our children the best of everything. Oftentimes, this includes paying additional money for a child's educational needs to make sure they have optimal learning experiences. We might pay for a private school, one-on-one tutoring, or extracurricular activities. Compound that with the fact that we live in a world of instant gratification and social media, and it's easy to see why parents feel the pinch when it comes to children and finances.

Raising children is a beautifully rewarding, albeit expensive, task. While I yet to have children of my own, I have seen firsthand the expenses that family and friends incur and how that can cut into one's spending plans. According to the Department of Agriculture, in order to raise a child from birth to the age of 17, it will cost a family an average of $233,610[2]. Like it or not, today's world is different. A shopping trip with my cousin to help pick out an outfit for her son's eighth-grade prom (you read that correctly—an eighth-grade prom) opened my eyes to how societal pressures are forcing parents to spend more than ever before. I remember how much of a financial burden I felt from my prom back in the early 2000s, and I was a junior in high school! Wearing a nice suit and tie just won't cut it anymore. The pressure to shine is more immense now that social media platforms are driving forces behind what is in and what is not. I watched in horror as kids were going all out with custom-made jackets and designer shoes (yes, the ones with the red soles) for a single event in eighth grade. If that was the eighth grade, I could only imagine what high school prom was going to look like in the future. Luckily, my cousin's son opted for something smart. He picked out inexpensive items that he could wear multiple times, thus making the purchase more practical in terms of cost per wear.

Parents and caregivers must keep in mind that spending excessively to provide children with great experiences and what you believe to be a great

START HERE

life isn't always ideal. In fact, extreme spending and the debt that comes with it can actually backfire. You might think the things and experiences you are going into debt for will improve your family dynamic, but you will likely find yourself weighed down with the debt more than anything. How many times have you found yourself stressed and financially maxed out after putting together the ultimate birthday party or Christmas for your child, only to discover that they're more interested in something that didn't cost you hardly anything? We've all seen that happen at family gatherings—the box is more interesting than the present that came in it.

Let's keep it real here. Most children don't realize they're missing out on something unless we tell them. Often, the beliefs that we have surrounding our children's perception of lack are projections from our own experiences. Are children truly missing out, or are you trying to recreate childhood memories for yourself? Most five-year-olds would be perfectly happy with a simple pizza party, trip to the movies, or a playdate with friends. A Christmas tree with a few well-intentioned gifts underneath it is just as special as one overflowing with presents. The excess that feels so important to us is a nonessential part of their happiness.

The number one influences on a child's financial behavior are their parents, with many Americans feeling that they learned the most about personal finances from their parents.[3,4] With children today having access to things that we would never have dreamed of, the importance of having age-appropriate financial conversations as early as possible cannot be emphasized enough.

These types of conversations allow children to learn basic lessons in financial literacy, and they can be done by using the family finances as an example. By weaving money lessons into day-to-day life, you have the ability to influence thoughts, values, and behavior surrounding money before outside influences start to insert themselves. As money conversations within the home become more commonplace, you may find that children are more inclined to be on board with helping the family reach financial goals if they can see the tangible benefit for themselves.

A dear friend of mine has been working diligently to prepare for her first home purchase. She openly shares this journey with her kids so that they are exposed to conversations surrounding finances at an early age. She shared a story with me about how her son was asking her almost daily about when they were going to move into their own home. She explained the process of home buying and saving money the best way anyone could to a seven-year-old. Afterward, he exclaimed, "Then we shouldn't have gone to Disneyland so we could have used that money for the house!" While this gave us both a good laugh, it also underscores the importance of family communication. At the young tender age of seven, her son was already willing to make sacrifices to help his family reach their financial goals.

One of the first steps you can take towards building a positive money mindset in your home is to stop treating finances as if it is a taboo subject that should only be discussed by adults behind closed doors. I'm not saying you have to share everything, as it is not your child's job to shoulder the weight of every financial concern. However, the conversations you do have when your child is young will create the foundation for a money-conscious adult.

Here are a couple of age-appropriate money lessons that you can teach your child at each stage to begin sculpting their positive money mindset. If you're not ready to dive into these lessons yet, mark this section to revisit at the end of the book as often as you and your family need it.

Preschool

Teach The Basics: You don't have to wait for your child to be able to count down from ten before introducing the basics of money. A child's numeracy development starts when they are newborns.[5] Even though they may not be able to tell you a coin's value, you can still incorporate number games that help children learn how to distinguish the differences among coins. You can then build upon this skill by playing number games that involve various coins and their value.

Give - Save - Spend: A great way for your child to begin to understand the various ways that money can be used is to teach money categories. At this tender age, the concepts of give, save, and spend allow a child to not only learn the importance of saving money for the future, but it also teaches empathy and allows children to think beyond themselves. When it comes to spending, I always consider this category to be a bonus. I look at it as a reward for making sure the first two tasks are complete. Spending is also a money lesson within itself. Not only does it reinforce the previous lesson on money basics by allowing them to count out how much they have, but it allows children to start making decisions on what they value. This lesson can also be continued with elementary-age children.

Elementary School

Upgrade the Piggy Bank: Nothing screams, "you've made it" like opening your first bank account. Although you'll probably still be using the Give-Save-Spend jars that you created when they were preschool age, opening a bank account is a chance for you to now start to gear money conversations around safe places to save and how to watch your money grow. Understandably, a child may still be too young to truly appreciate the concept surrounding the power of compounding. If we're honest here, brick and mortar banks aren't making history with the APYs on interest rates, but there are still great lessons to be taught through bank accounts.

Reward the Extraordinary: This may be a bit controversial, but I don't believe that children should receive an allowance for doing things that are expected of them. Good grades are expected. Cleaning your room and doing household chores, expected. One way I plan to circumvent this when I have children of my own is by rewarding their extraordinary achievements. Extraordinary achievements don't have to be *that* extraordinary. I'm not worried about having the first child to walk on the moon. Instead, these achievements can be instances that highlight a child's character, such as times they go above and beyond what is asked. For example, volunteering to help with the dishes without being asked or by being a Good Samaritan to someone in need are extraordinary. When I was younger, I used to love raking leaves. Don't ask me why. For me, it was just fun. One day, I went out and attempted to rake the leaves in our front yard without even being asked. Later that day, my stepfather surprised me by giving me $20 because he was proud that I took the initiative to help with the yard. Rewarding the extraordinary is a great way to teach children that hard work is oftentimes rewarded. What an important way to show them that they should always strive to do their best even when they think someone isn't watching.

Middle School

Help Them Discover Values: Most of us can probably agree that middle school is a preamble for high school. It is equal parts challenging and exciting. The mind is aflutter with new feelings as they start to figure out who they are, where they belong, and what they should be doing. This transitional period is a great time to have money focused on values. This is the time to show them that what they spend their money on is a reflection of the things that are currently important to them. As middle schoolers, they can be impressionable. Value-driven conversations can make the transition to high school smoother, as that is a time when students can really be swayed by outside influences if they aren't in tune with their own values.

Raising money smart kids means trusting them with the freedom to use their spending money how they want. However, we also want them to start thinking more strategically on whether or not their spending really brings them joy or if they're just doing it because everyone else is doing it. You can do this by asking probing questions about how they envision their future. Find out what things get them excited. If you've noticed, they've taken a particular interest in something, find out how much more they want to explore that area. With the provided answers, talk about how they can align their spending to bring these things to life. For instance, if they'd like a car by the time they turn sixteen, you can teach them that it's never too early to set specific savings goals. Show them how much money they are spending on things they don't necessarily care about and how quickly that money can add up if it were saved instead. By discovering what they value at an early age, they will be less prone to impulse spending that is influenced by others.

Fill Them In: When I was in middle school, I remember my mom coming home with a big bag of clothing. The bags were nondescript and revealed nothing that gave away where they came from. However, inside the bags were tons of clothes. Dresses, skirts, blazers, pants, you name it. I was on cloud nine as I laid out each item assuring, my mom that they would fit without even trying them on. I couldn't bear the possibility of her taking them back and me being left without. Once I started trying them on, I continually asked her where she got them. She would never give me an answer. She'd just smile or ask me why it mattered. I remember trying to look at the price tags on the clothing to see if they'd reveal the secret location of Mom's shopping spree, but they were about as non-descript as the bags. Eventually, it hit me that she got the clothes from Goodwill. I realized she didn't want to tell me where she got them from, possibly for fear that I may reject them. Although I realized that the clothes came from Goodwill, I didn't care one bit. New or new-to-me didn't matter. I couldn't wait to wear my new skirt with the matching jacket to church on Sunday.

At this age, the money conversations you will be having with your child are maturing just as they are. Although you've done your best to protect them from those "hard" financial conversations surrounding bills and debt, this is the perfect time to start sharing the benefits of frugality. My mom revealing where she got the clothes from could have gone two ways. I could have reacted by sneering my nose up at them in disgust, followed by a lesson in contentment. I also could have shown her that I understood the reason behind her choosing to shop at Goodwill over a department store. A conversation on these choices would have been a great segue for a discussion on what is called opportunity cost. By choosing to save money on clothes, she was able to fund something else that I possibly desired or even needed. Another great conversation could center on the fact that material things and their price tags don't determine our worth as people.

If you want to explore self-worth more with your child, have the child list all the things that make them the amazing person they are. Once their list is complete, have them circle all the things that are material factors versus ones that are character traits. Highlight that even without those material things, they would still be the amazing person that you love and care about.

High School

The Anatomy of A Paycheck: In the eyes of a teenager, securing a part-time job probably fits right up there with getting your driver's license. It means responsibility, independence, and freedom. It also means a paycheck! More than likely, your teen has probably come up with numerous ways to spend their first paycheck. They have big plans until they actually receive their check and come to the stark realization that there is this thing called taxes. I still remember bawling my eyes out in my mom's car after receiving my first paycheck from my part-time job at the newly opened McAlister's Deli. This is when my mom explained to me how taxes worked and why I had to pay Social Security. I felt robbed! After working all those hours, I couldn't believe that I wasn't entitled to every penny that I'd earn. Before your teenager picks up a part-time

START HERE

job in an establishment that will issue them a paycheck, find examples of paychecks online and walk through each area so that they have a full understanding of what to expect when they receive theirs. To run through different scenarios, use a paycheck calculating site like paycheckcity.com, which will allow you and your teen to estimate what their check will look like each pay period before they receive it.

The Do's and Don'ts of Debit Cards: It's inevitable that your teen will need to use a debit card or have access to a credit card. According to a 2019 survey by T.Rowe Price, 17% of kids ages 8-14 have a credit card.[6] As much as we'd like to think that they'll be responsible, here is where you don't want to leave anything to chance by keeping them uninformed. Teach them how to wield it properly by having conversations early on to help them better understand what debit cards are, how they work, and the consequences for abusing them. You can start by having them use their debit card only when you are around, and then walking them through their online bank accounts to show them the effects of their spending. Use this time to set boundaries around their debit card use and clarify what happens if your teen overspends.

When teaching financial lessons to teenagers, one of my favorite things to do is use a check reconciliation sheet and teach them how to balance their "checkbooks" the old fashioned way. Using a list of expenses, I have them complete the exercise by telling me how much money they have leftover after all debits and credits are taken into account. Unbeknownst to them, I secretly set it up so that they will fall into the negative and start to accrue fees. This allows me to teach a valuable lesson in how they should pay close attention to the money coming in and money coming out at all times to avoid overspending and paying heavily for the mistake. While apps are great tools for helping your teen stay on track with their spending, nothing beats seeing the effects of your spending in real time and making those calculations by hand. This is also a great way to explain other nuances that go along with having a debit card like what it means to overdraft and the fees they'll be charged, the long term effects of having delinquent accounts, the delay in credits or debits posting, and how to use a debit card safely to avoid identity theft and being scammed. If you find that your teenager is becoming too swipe-happy or isn't particularly ready for a debit card, switch to cash or use a prepaid card until they are ready for the responsibility of using a debit card.

College

Student Loans: Although I am forever grateful to my alma mater North Carolina A&T State University, there are times when I look at my student loans and wish my parents *forced* me to take a more affordable route for getting an education. Conversations surrounding student loans should take place well before your child enters college and continue while they are in college. As of 2018, $1.5 trillion dollars is owed in student loan debt making it the second largest source of consumer debt in the United States.[7] I probably don't have to tell you that the effects of the student loan crisis have been staggering. It has caused delays in saving for retirement, purchasing homes, and even starting families. This information should not be glossed over when having discussions surrounding student loans with your child. Entrance and exit counseling are not and have never been enough to educate a new college student on the responsibilities for having a student loan. Have your child do the math up front so they have a true understanding of how much school will cost them. Walk through the scenario of them making an average starting salary in their field of interest and how student loan payments could possibly affect their quality of living. To avoid fear-mongering, show scenarios on both sides of the fence. Set guidelines for how much you can contribute to their education and how much they will be responsible for themselves.

You can also discuss alternative paths for paying for an education. While grants and scholarships should be at the top of your list, don't be

START HERE

afraid to bring up starting at a community college or going to trade schools as viable and celebrated options that will still allow your child to achieve their desired education. You can also pursue other online and low-cost alternatives, as well as look into certification versus degree programs.

Navigating Credit Cards: Most college kids are thrown head first into credit cards 101 upon entering college. That means they are starting their transition into the use of plastic at a very early age. Out of 30,000 college students across 45 states, a survey sponsored by AIG found that almost half of those students had at least one credit card. That same survey found 61% of that group acquired their cards when they were 18 years old or younger.[8]

Having money conversations surrounding obtaining a credit card and the pros and cons of using one can save you and them a lot of agony in the future. As credit is borrowed money, it's important that they understand the ramifications on the cost of the items charged to the card when they don't pay their balance in full each. Discuss topics like Truth In Lending and The Card Act, which requires financial institutions and businesses to disclose vital information when issuing new credit cards. Discuss the importance of always paying the bill on time as well as minimum payments, APR, and how credit card usage can affect one's credit score. All of these things can have long-term effects on a young adult's financial situation for years or even decades to come.

Establishing a positive money mindset within yourself allows you to pass your financially conscious traits on to your children. This is the start of building generational wealth. We often catch ourselves saying, "I was never taught that!" when it comes to money topics. Don't give your kids a reason to grow up saying the same things. Money conscious kids grow into money conscious adults. Don't worry if your children are beyond that young tender age where they'll happily listen to what you have to say.

PARENTAL PERSUASION

Look for ways to have money conversations in a way that is appealing to your adolescent or young adult. Share news articles about money featuring some of their favorite celebrities. If you don't feel comfortable having these money conversations, get them engaged in programs that teach financial literacy. There are often in-person programs at libraries, community centers, and churches. Plus, a quick online search will reveal dozens of self-paced online learning opportunities.

Although you may not be able to afford to give your children all the things you wish they could have, you can instill traditions that allow them to experience the abundance of life while keeping in line with your money values. Paired with age-appropriate conversations on financial literacy, these traditions and lessons will hopefully last a lifetime.

Get Into the Game

Living Broke on Purpose is a team effort for my husband and me. But I have to be 100% honest—my husband wasn't always pulling his fair share of the weight as part of the team when Broke on Purpose first started. Now, I don't say this to throw him under the bus; I say this because women who are married or in serious relationships almost always ask the same question: "How do I get my spouse or significant other on board with getting our finances and order and wanting to pay off debt?" I wish I could tell you that there was some magic spell you could mumble that would make your spouse just as excited about transforming your finances as you currently are, but there isn't. While he had committed to combining incomes, he hadn't fully committed to being a co-supervisor of our money. I would do the budget, I would pay the bills, and he would just go along with it.

He was on cruise control.

As long as nothing major popped up, he didn't feel a need to be bothered.

While this may not be as extreme as some relationships, it was serious to me.

In order for us to really tackle this debt the way I knew we could, I had to get my husband on the same page as me. While I was doing it alone and doing it well (pops collar), I couldn't continue to carry the burden alone. When we reached a milestone, I would tell him about it, highlighting his efforts and contributions. I would show my excitement and ask him to share in the excitement with me. Most times, I would get a less than enthusiastic "That's great!" from him, but I didn't let it deter me.

To say I never got upset wouldn't be truthful. There have been a few occasions where I let my husband know how his nonchalant attitude was doing more harm than good. He couldn't be an ex-football player and coach who preached "Team Work, Motivation, Determination, and Persistence" on the field and then completely forget about those values off the field -to me, paying off debt needed to be a team effort. We were Team Wright and we were up against Team Debt in the biggest game of our financial lives. As a team, we were trying to get into the other team's end zone and score every month. Not a month goes by that we're not met with obstacles, so I needed someone to be on that offensive line with me. I had to get him to see that I couldn't keep scoring these points by myself without getting injured mentally.

When you embark on any journey towards debt payoff or financial independence, it can often feel like one of the longest journeys of your life. You're going to need someone to help keep you motivated or someone you can tag in. You need to be surrounded by a team that has your back. You don't have to be married or in a serious relationship to experience the benefit of teamwork. If you're single, this type of teamwork can come in the form of family, friends, or an accountability partner to keep you motivated and help you stay on track. This person acts as a sounding board,

START HERE

telling you when you're wrong and celebrating with you when you've hit a milestone no matter the size.

If you're in a serious relationship or married, teamwork is going to include all those things above and a little bit more. One of my favorite examples of teamwork comes from the movie *300*. The way those Spartan soldiers worked in unison to fight against their enemy, who often outnumbered them, was a spellbinding thing to see. Let's be honest; they didn't look half bad either! Each soldier complemented the other. They knew each other's strengths and weaknesses so well that they were able to work together as one impenetrable force.

This level of collaboration is the type of teamwork you're going to need if you want to make a change with your family finances. No more "that's his debt" or "she ran up the credit card bill." Leave the accusations and the individual debt ownership in the past. You now have one common goal: Change the financial landscape of your family. You're going to work together to save, fund your dreams, pay off debt, and create a life where there is always money left over. If you're single, you're going to be doing exactly the same thing.

It's never fun going up against an opponent who is bigger and stronger than you are, and sometimes that's how battling debt feels. Trust me—you won't win this game by throwing your weight around or talking smack (I've tried and failed). You'll have to be cunning, staying one step ahead at all times. You're going to be pushed and tested in ways you never imagined. There will be times when it may feel like nothing is working out in your favor. You take two steps forward and wind up taking, three steps back.

The stakes have never been higher. Your entire life is going to transform. Even when you're on the right track, you'll notice the difficulties, obstacles, and the exhausting effort required. During such a transformation, you'll find yourself more in tune with the negative things happening around you. What you don't realize is that these things have been happening all along.

Because you allowed them to coexist with you in your life, they never felt threatening before. Keep fighting now.

The key to winning is to show up ready to face your opponents—debt, delinquencies, negative balances, late fees. Come to the game prepared with an offensive playbook so strong that no matter what your opponents throw at you, you can stand confident knowing there's a play for that. Here are four plays that should always be in your financial playbook— the vision play, the conversation play, the in-agreement, and the all-in play.

The Vision Play - A personal understanding of your attitudes and values around money. What is important to you, and why is it important to you? This play allows you to have a clear understanding of the things that are important in your life.

The Conversation Play - The ability to have respectful, open, and honest dialogue without criticism, anger, or judgment. If you are single, these are the conversational boundaries you'll set with your family, friends, and accountability partners.

The In-Agreement Play - The willingness to evaluate the entire situation and make a decision based on what is best for the financial household instead of what benefits you most individually.

The All-In Play - The willingness to do your part no matter what to make the financial plan work.

Remember that woman who talked about getting her finances together but never actually did it? Neither does anyone else. Do you know how many times I said to myself, "Melody, today you're going to commit to getting your finances together," but never actually did it? I can tell you this: That number exceeds the number of fingers that I have on both hands. Starting and stopping is something you do when you're driving, not when you're serious about making a change with your finances.

START HERE

You have a choice to make. Either you're going to do this, or this is going to be another book that sits dusty on your shelf. The choice is yours, and I can't make it for you. What I can do is remind you that your dreams are valid, they're within reach, and you have to make up your mind whether or not you're going to take the required steps to go after them. Are you going to be part of the team or a spectator in the crowd?

BUILD YOUR MONEY MANAGEMENT SYSTEM

You Don't Always Have to Work Harder

I received one of the best pieces of advice while working on my master's in Animal Health Science. I'd been struggling in the lab, trying to get an immunological assay to work. It would have been easy to blame the problems on the kit not working, but my mentor had already successfully tested it, so we knew that the issue was more than likely user error—that user being me. Because we had limited resources, my mentor offered to come and observe to see if she could identify what I may have been doing wrong. The assay had a lot of steps and several moving pieces. While one part was incubating, I had to be preparing for the next phase of the experiment. As she watched me work, she notated several areas of possible error introduction. She also noted how much time I spent running back and forth, collecting reagents to prepare fresh solutions, labeling tubes, setting up equipment, and so on. I wish I could tell you that we figured out why the assay wasn't working, but honestly, I don't remember. I probably don't remember because her advice trumped everything else that happened that day. It made a lightbulb go off that changed the way I approached things from then on out. That advice went like this: "You have to learn

YOU DON'T ALWAYS HAVE TO WORK HARDER

how to work smarter, not harder." Working smart and working hard go hand in hand, but if you take the time to map out how you're going to approach a challenge, you give yourself the upper hand.

Your finances have a lot of moving parts. Just like in my assay, each one of those moving pieces can potentially introduce errors or confusion into your plan. As you move through this book, I want you to apply the same piece of advice my mentor gave me to your finances. I want you to approach your money from a position of working smarter, not harder. This will call for you to find the connection between the money you have and the life you want to live. To do this, I'm going to provide you with the blueprint for creating a strategic Money Management System. This System will help you plan, allowing you to put your money in a position to work hard while you reap all the benefits. That's smart!

Now, before we dive into this section, I want to warn you that we're going to cover a lot of ground. You may start to feel that things are becoming a bit overwhelming or that maybe you aren't cut out for making this financial change at all. Think of all those things that you're a master at now. Did you start off being great at them, or did it take time for you to perfect that skill? Of course, it took time. Money is no different. To perfect your finances, you have to start somewhere. Think of this beginning as your fresh start. Here is where you learn the skills, acquire the tools, and map out your plan of action. Turning back will only put you right back where you started. Pushing through introduces you to a whole new level of possibility. Let's do this!

A Money Management What?

Learning how to manage your money confidently is the key to living an abundant life. Our circumstances can make us feel as though we never have enough or that we have to make more money to live the life that we want. In reality, for many, what it comes down to isn't making more; it's managing the money we do have better.

Finances aren't a singular thing. Several moving pieces work together behind the scenes. When you think about it in terms of a big-picture view, your finances run just like a system. A system performs its functions through input, processes, and output. Something goes in, things happen, and then, after what seems like a magical transformation, something appears on the other side.

There are systems all around us. Some we see, some we don›t. Inside of our bodies, there are essential systems, like the respiratory system, to help us breathe and the circulatory system that supplies the body with nutrients, blood, and oxygen. The postal system allows us to deliver mail from one zip code to another efficiently. The transportation system works to maintain structure around how we move about in this world. Last but

A MONEY MANAGEMENT WHAT?

not least, Chick-Fil-A has an amazing drive-thru system that allows us to order our food in a swift and efficient process. What these examples have in common is that they are made up of individual pieces that are interconnected to provide an optimal desired output.

Although it may not seem like it, your finances run similarly to the systems that I just described. This is why I call it a Money Management System. As money flows into your life, multiple things are happening in the background and foreground that are responsible for the output that you see. The most important question is whether or not that output is something you actually want.

Your Money Management System is made up of several stations that act as their own individual systems. They are a system within a system. Each of these stations is interconnected. They also run off of their own set of rules and responsibilities that help you work toward reaching your predefined financial goals. Imagine one big factory with different stations doing their own set of processes and procedures to help meet the final goal of pushing out the product. If one of these stations goes down or has an error, every other station is affected.

These efficient systems aren't made overnight. To make my financial system work, I had to reframe my viewpoint. Instead of seeing myself as separate from my finances, I chose to look at the interconnectedness of it all. There are parts of me that love planning, organization, structure, and automation. By focusing on these attributes, I knew I could take control of my finances. In fact, I no longer saw my finances as a big mess or huge obstacle; I could finally see how each part of them and each quality of myself could work together to improve my money management. While the attributes that I described may not necessarily be the best identifiers for you, as we begin to create your Money Management System, you'll start to see how you can mold it to fit your idiosyncrasies and characteristics.

Now, I want you to think back to a time when a system hit a snag.

START HERE

One of my favorite examples of this comes from an old TV sitcom called *I Love Lucy*. In this particular episode, Lucy was working on the line in a chocolate factory. She was tasked with the role of wrapping each piece of chocolate before it got to the packing room. At first, things seemed pretty easy, and she was able to successfully wrap the candy as it came down the line. To her surprise, the conveyor belt suddenly sped up, sending the candy down the line faster than she was able to wrap them. Unprepared, Lucy tried her best to wrap as many as she could. To keep the unwrapped candy from making its way into the packing room, she found herself stuffing chocolate in her mouth or down her dress. It was a catastrophe! As a result of this mishap, one can imagine the packing area didn't receive its wrapped candies, resulting in a backup of the entire line!

Not familiar with the show *I Love Lucy*? Take the transportation system as another example. What happens when a traffic light goes out? What about when people fail to follow the traffic laws? Chaos ensues, traffic backs up for miles, and the resulting output is anything but favorable. The same thing happens with your finances! When something inside your Money Management System isn't functioning as it should, it can put a wrench in the rest of your financial plans.

Now, imagine if everything worked accurately and seamlessly. What if your money could flow through your Money Management System in such a way that it helped you to relieve stress, save time, and focus on all the other things you love about life?

Before I show you how to set up this personal finance management system, let›s briefly walk through each station of your Money Management System.

Income Station - Your income is the raw, unrefined product that goes into your Money Management System. Your income is the amount of money you bring in. It can be from your full-time job, part-time job, side

A MONEY MANAGEMENT WHAT?

hustle, passive income, or windfalls and gifts.

Budget/Spending Plan Station - The Budget/Spending Plan Station is the income recruitment center. It takes your income and gives it a purpose and role to fill within the system.

The Living Station- This station houses the Essential Spending Department and Non-Essential Spending Department. The Essential Spending Department is in charge of all the spending that is essential to your survival. The Non-Essential Spending Department is in charge of all the spending that, while adding comfort to life, is not needed to survive on a day-to-day basis.

The Savings Station: This station houses the Retirement Savings Department and the Non-Retirement Savings Department. The Retirement Savings Department holds all the savings for your non-job related retirement accounts, like your IRA, Roth IRA, investments, stocks, and bonds. If you are self-employed, this station will also house your self-employed retirement vehicles. The Non-Retirement Savings Department handles your short-term and long-term saving plans, along with providing maintenance on your emergency fund.

Debt Station - The debt station manages your debt and any debt repayment plans and strategies you may have in place.

Use the next chapters as a blueprint for creating your own Money Management System. I'll break down each station and walk you through some important processes and procedures that can help the area run smoothly. Though it may be tempting to jump ahead to the station you want to work on most, make sure you build out each station in the order that they are shown. Once you've completed the framework for your system, feel free to go back to finetune or adjust as needed.

Remember, your Money Management System is not something you can build once and forget. It's going to need consistent maintenance to

START HERE

make sure it's running efficiently. You may find that there will be times when you need to reduce the flow of income to some sections or completely shut them down so that money can be realigned elsewhere. This is okay, as the system is designed to function based on your current needs.

Take some time to review the diagram of the Money Management System below. As you continue reading, refer back to the picture to help you visualize how the system is linked and how they can work together to help you accomplish your financial goals.

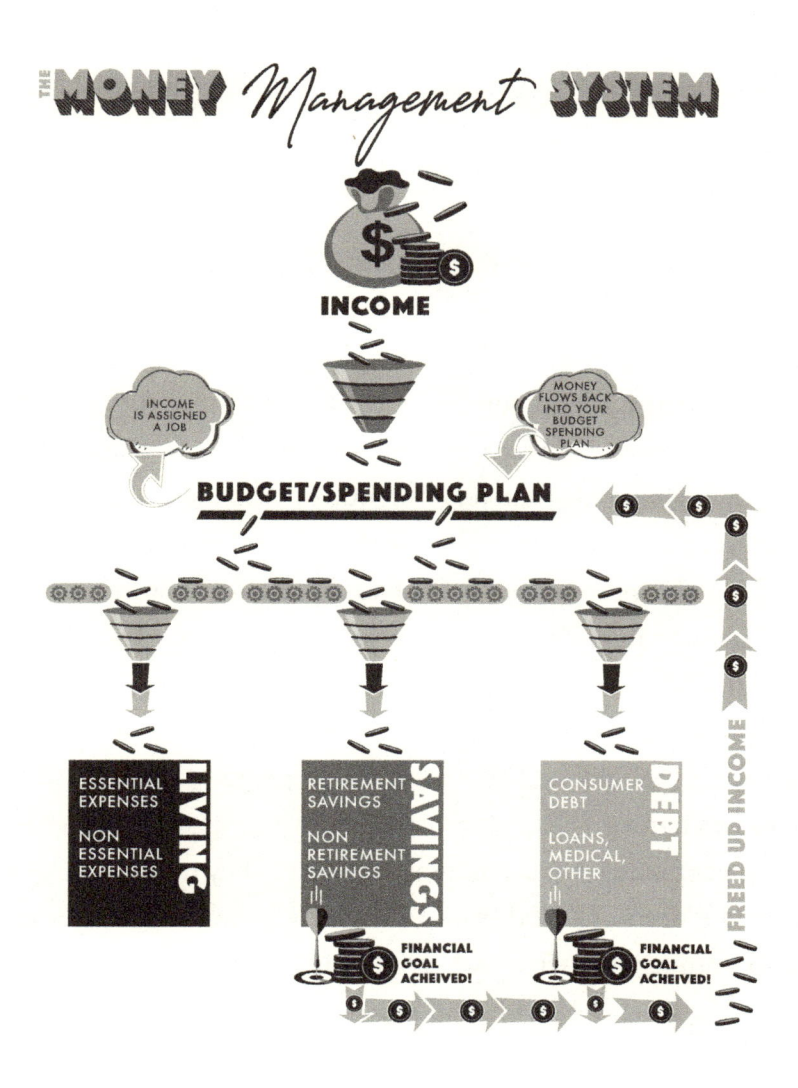

THE MONEY Management SYSTEM

INCOME

Income is assigned a job

Money flows back into your budget spending plan

BUDGET/SPENDING PLAN

LIVING
- ESSENTIAL EXPENSES
- NON ESSENTIAL EXPENSES

SAVINGS
- RETIREMENT SAVINGS
- NON RETIREMENT SAVINGS

FINANCIAL GOAL ACHEIVED!

DEBT
- CONSUMER DEBT
- LOANS, MEDICAL, OTHER

FINANCIAL GOAL ACHEIVED!

FREED UP INCOME

It Starts With Why

Now that you have an idea of how a Money Management System works, the next step is to decide what you want your system to produce. What is your desired output? There are a lot of so-called rules in the world of personal finance. With something as important as your finances, it's understandable that you want to make sure that you're doing everything correctly to ensure the best possible outcome. In short, rule following makes sense. But there's a problem with these rules. Many of these rules leave a lot of people unsure of what to do when it comes to creating a financial plan or uncertain about how to set goals in a way that reflects their dream life.

Now, I am proposing a whole new way of looking at your finances with a system behind it. The reason many people look toward specific resources and hard-set rules to structure their finances is that they have yet to create clear financial goals that inspire them. They might have goals, but they lack the desire to work toward achieving them! Having a financial goal of becoming debt-free isn't as fulfilling as sharing the why behind it. The *why* is special—it is full of emotion, dreams, and stories. It's that

START HERE

special reason that makes you get out of bed before the alarm goes off to get to work early or to work that extra shift even though you're exhausted.

It's important to talk about your *why*. I'll share mine first. At one point, my *why* was that I simply wanted to feel like I could breathe when I thought about our financial situation. It was the longing to feel like there was enough of our money to go around and allow us to live. It didn't matter that my idea of living was the ability to order pizza on a Friday night once a month. It wasn't the most extravagant reason, but it was important to me. It was one of the results that I wanted from my Money Management System.

When setting up your Money Management System, you have to know what the final output is going to be and why it matters. Why is it so important that all these separate units work together? What is waiting on the other side? What's your why? If you need help coming up with something, these questions will help you.

1. If you could change anything about your finances, what would it be?
2. Why is the answer above so important to you? Why do you want to accomplish this?
3. How would you feel once this is accomplished?
4. What would you be willing to do, sacrifice, or change in order for it to happen?

Allow these answers to come together and form your why. You're not reading this book just because you want to learn a little more information about your finances. You're reading it because you need something to happen, to shift, and to transform. You want to feel the freedom, joy, and security that having a Money Management System in place will give you. Your why might be to pay for your child's college education, to take your mom on a dream vacation, or maybe to breathe. Whatever it is, keep it at the forefront of your mind as we start to build out your Money Management System.

Mentally Manageable Pieces

Think of your life as one big road map and think of your financial goals as a list of landmarks that you encounter along the way. There's no specific order in which you should stop and visit each site. Just like if you were to use your GPS, you'd find there are multiple ways to get where you want to go. Of course, you could get in your car and just drive, but driving aimlessly can often result in you turning down a one-way street, heading toward a particular place you don't want to be. You need a roadmap, a recipe, or a protocol. Whatever you want to call it, you need something that you can follow that will take you from point A to point Z. Your job is to look at your financial goals in relation to where you are in your life and where you want to be. Then, you need to figure out which of the many possible steps makes sense to stop at next.

Even if you know your why, writing out your financial goals can be a daunting experience, especially when your sole focus is wanting to get out of debt or quickly cleaning up a financial mess so that you can move on with your life. You'll find that your goals vary in size. Some of them are going to be easy to complete, while others are going to make you feel like

MENTALLY MANAGEABLE PIECES

you're going up against the final boss in your favorite video game and you have none of the tools to defeat him.

I still remember the crippling anxiety I would feel each time I looked at our student loans. I would end up just turning off the computer and walking away. I just didn't need that type of negativity in my life. In all honesty, our student loans turned out to be a huge mental roadblock for me. I realized that because our debt was so massive, I would find myself getting dissuaded by the number, instead of looking at ways to tackle it. It didn't matter that I knew how much I wanted to pay them off. I kept shutting down instead of creating a system to get started.

I was finally able to work past the anxiety of our overall student loan debt when I stopped fixating on that one landmark and turned my focus to the entire road map. There were so many places I could go. I didn't have to start at my student loans! When I was ready and more equipped, I could make a U-turn and go back to them. To be successful, I had to break my financial goals down into mentally manageable pieces by focusing on what I could do at that current point. I had to stop using today's solutions for tomorrow's problems. By doing this, I wouldn't risk clogging up my Money Management System with delays by tackling things I wasn't ready to tackle.

Breaking down your financial goals into mentally manageable pieces allows you to focus on what you can handle at this moment. We often find ourselves pulled in many different directions due to jobs, families, and other obligations in life. Finding time to focus on another big responsibility can be hard. Look at the landmarks on your roadmap and ask yourself this question:

What can I handle today, and why is it so important for me to get this done?

START HERE

Mentally manageable goals give you the psychological and emotional space to deal with whatever task lies ahead successfully. Think of what you want to accomplish at each landmark and break it down into the action steps required to make it all come together.

Step 1: Start by writing down each landmark. Think about what you want to do when you get there. For instance, your first landmark could be that you want to call a creditor and ask them to move your payment date to one that is more convenient for you.

Step 2: Next, set a date for when you want to accomplish this task. Our example of moving a payment date is one of the easier goals, so you should be able to accomplish it in a relatively short amount of time. If it takes you longer than a week to get this done, you should probably have another "come to Jesus" meeting with yourself.

Step 3: Now, ask yourself, "Why is this important?" Let's return to our previous example: Calling to adjust your date is important because you are less likely to miss a payment by moving the payment to right after your payday.

Step 4: For the final step, make it a declaration that helps you feel empowered to complete the goal.

Here's how all four steps sound when they're put together: *I am going to call my creditor and ask them to move my payment due date by the end of the week. By having the payment moved closer to the date I get paid, it will reduce the likelihood of me missing or making the payment late.*

Walk-through the list of financial goals you've made and break down the ones that scare you into mentally manageable pieces, like the one shown above. If the goal still seems too big after you've broken it down, keep breaking it down until you feel like you can confidently take action.

If your goals still feel too intimidating, there's a different approach you can try called reverse engineering. Reverse engineering is the concept

MENTALLY MANAGEABLE PIECES

of taking completed work and deconstructing it. Essentially, by picking a finished product apart, you reveal how the item was made. It's like finding a plan of action in reverse. Reverse engineering is an older practice that is becoming more commonly used in the tech world when companies want to know how a competitor's product is designed.

Now, let's apply reverse engineering to our finances. Let's say your goal is to pay off $10,000 of your student loan debt this year. To come up with a plan of action through reverse engineering, start by pulling the layers of the goal apart. Think of it like pulling back the peel on a banana.

Ask yourself probing questions like:
- How does someone usually go about achieving a goal like this?
- How much will it take to pay this off in a certain amount of time?
- Who do I need to call for more information or advice?
- Which repayment method will work best?
- Are there particular mindsets or habits required to achieve a goal like this? If so, how can I make them a part of my life?

As you come up with the answers, write them down in your money journal and arrange them in such a way that they create a roadmap that could potentially take you from the start all the way to the end of your goal.

Demystifying Your Net Worth

Now that you've determined the desired output of your Money Management System and set financial goals, it's now time to analyze what you are currently working with. You need to determine the level at which your current framework for money management is operating.

Goals are essential; however, setting a goal doesn't mean that you're starting at the very beginning. You'd be surprised how many people set goals only to find that they were actually already three-quarters of the way to the finish line. The reason they could never see this before is that there was no true structure in place to tell them how they were progressing. There was too much noise getting in the way.

One of the quickest ways to determine how you stand financially in relation to your goals and your overall financial health is to calculate your net worth. Knowing your net worth allows you to see the big picture of your finances and allows you to create the foundation where you can live as richly as you want. In a nutshell, your net worth is assets minus liabilities. To calculate your net worth, start by totaling your assets. Said another way, make a tally of everything you own. Then, subtract your liabilities, which are the things you owe money on. The final number allows you to quickly assess whether you're behind schedule, on track, or ahead of the game.

Now that you know how it's done, it's time for you to crunch the numbers. Make a list of all your assets and liabilities. Take time to look things up if you don't know the numbers offhand. Creating a list ensures that nothing gets left behind. You may also be able to use this list for other financial planning exercises that you'll be completing as you make your way through this book.

After you've done the math, there are some things to keep in mind. I want you to remember that your net worth does not equal your self-worth. It is a number, but it is not who we are as people. Another thing to note is not be surprised if you find yourself with a negative net worth. Negative net worths are typical among people who are still carrying large amounts of student loan debt or other personal debts. According to a study from the Deloitte Group, the net worth for ages 18-35 has dropped 34% since 1996.[9] The reasons behind this finding have nothing to do with the fact that this age range consists of Millennials. (Let's be honest, they'd blame an alien invasion on Millennials if they could.) Instead, reasons do include stagnant wages, soaring education costs, and overall increases in the cost of living.

There's something else to consider as well. Different people have different feelings about liabilities. Take us for instance. With all that we've paid off and accomplished over the last few years, our assets have yet to be more than our liabilities. Not all liabilities are bad. Sometimes, we take on liabilities because we know that they have the potential to create assets. Student loans are a great example of this. My student loans are my biggest liability, yet they are also what one could consider to be an *invisible* asset. Invisible assets are defined as assets that cannot be seen or touched, but still provide value to the holder. Because I am not working in the scientific field, my student loans aren't generating income in such

START HERE

a way that they will eventually be paid off from that income. However, while I may no longer be practicing science as a full-time career, I still use the skills that I cultivated every single day. On paper, your student loans, medical debt, car payments obligations may evoke feelings of regret; however, if you approach certain liabilities from an abundance mindset, you shift those feelings to ones where you can appreciate the invisible assets those liabilities provide.

Take some time and plug your numbers into the net worth calculator below. Should there be a category missing from either the assets or liabilities columns, be sure to include it into your calculations. Remember, your net worth is not your self-worth. Use the information to help you shape your financial goals and the desired output of your Money Management System.

NET WORTH

ASSETS		LIABILITIES	
CASH		CONSUMER DEBT	
CHECKING ACCOUNTS		AUTO LOANS	
SAVINGS ACCOUNTS		MORTGAGE	
REAL ESTATE		STUDENT LOANS	
RETIREMENT ACCOUNTS		PERSONAL LOANS	
AUTOMOBILES		HOME EQUITY LOANS	
INVESTMENTS		COLLECTIONS	
OTHER		OTHER	

TOTAL ASSETS $_____

(-) TOTAL LIABILITIES $_____

= NET WORTH $_____

The Income Station

Income is often described as a tool that you can use to shape your financial future. While this viewpoint is correct, I also like to look at my income as raw material. From that perspective, the options available for how I use my income become the tools that help me mold this material into precisely what I desire it to be.

Income is important. On a global level, it's so important that the world uses it to determine socioeconomic status and to provide access to various facets of life unequally. On a personal level, it's the fuel and driving force of your Money Management System. Like a car that doesn't have any gas, there would be nothing for your system to run on without income.

You do not need a huge income for your Money Management System to run efficiently. Instead, think of it as quality over quantity. It's also imoortant to note that the amount of your income flowing into your Money Management System isn't directly proportional to the speed at which your Money Management System runs. A larger income would help you reach some financial goals faster, however it's not required for the Money Management System to function. Larger incomes don't always

START HERE

equate to automatic success. Typically, when you have less of something, you're more likely to take the necessary steps to make the most of it. I've been on both sides of the fence. There have been times when I had a substantial income and times when I was barely scraping by. During those times, when I was making a modest income, I was more focused on where my money was going, how it got there, and how my financial goals looked. Once my income increased, I enjoyed making more money. Conversely, I didn't feel as in tune with how my Money Management System was working. The simple fact is that my ego led me to believe that I had enough to make it work without being as conscientious as I was when I made less. To avoid falling into the complacent mindset, consider yourself the head supervisor of your Money Management System. It is up to you to do consistent checks and balances to ensure your income flows into and throughout your Money Management System as you've planned.

Your Spending Habits Are a Mirror

"Show me your bank statement, and I'll show you what you value."
-Unknown

The more I spent money, the more I found myself feeling that I had to make more money. Have you ever had that feeling? Have you ever felt like you didn't make enough despite knowing your salary was decent? Usually, the culprit behind this feeling lies in how we handle the money that's coming in. Your income is being siphoned away before it has a chance to make its way through your Money Management System. Want to know where your money is going? Nine times out of ten, the answer can be found in your spending. Your spending is a reflection of the things that you value. It shows what takes precedence in your life. If you looked at my spending before, I started living Broke on Purpose, you would immediately be able to tell that I valued makeup, clothes, Dunkin' Donuts coffee, the occasional sit-down restaurant, and making continuous credit card payments. You wouldn't find consistent deposits into my savings account or Roth IRA because they didn't fall in line with what I valued at the time.

START HERE

Knowing what you value and bringing your spending into an agreement with those values, allows your income to easily make it to the next station in your Money Management System. It's about getting clear on what you truly want out of life so that the habits and triggers going on around you don't obscure your view about what's important. For example, if you value travel, allow your money to flow safely into the Non-Retirement section of your Savings Station to save up for your next trip, instead of letting it be swiped away by an impulse purchase of a new handbag.

In a financial empowerment session with a client who was feeling like she was struggling with figuring out where her money was going, I had her describe what a perfect day would look like if money wasn't a consideration. Her eyes lit up as she talked about her love for fiber arts. She talked at length about how she would purchase equipment to help her process more wool and spin her own yarn. I then asked her if her current spending habits were helping her make that perfect day come true or if they were getting in the way of seeing that day come to fruition. She valued the arts, she valued her community, and she valued being able to share her gifts with the world. Her spending, though, was painting a different picture.

Think about your own spending. Is it in line with your perfect day, perfect year, or perfect life?

Habits, Trends, and Triggers

There are influences all around us. Many of us have been consciously and subconsciously influenced by family, community, music, social media, and many other factors. These influences play a significant role in our attitude towards finances. In fact, when you think about the choices you make with your money, it's easy to recall past experiences that have shaped your perception and the way you choose to live. Our nonessential spending is impacted by three categories of influence: habits, trends, and triggers.

HABITS are routine behaviors that are often subconscious. We all have habits, both good and bad. Have you ever thought about how your habits can contribute to the state of your finances?

One of the most detrimental habits discussed in the world of personal finance is the need to stop and pick up coffee every morning. It's also been dubbed The Latte Factor. There's a debate as to whether or not this action actually harms your finances. No matter which side of the debate you land on, spending five dollars a day on coffee (or anything else!) can add up. I'm not going to tell you to give up coffee, but I am going to ask you how it falls in line with the things you value. One of the habits that I picked

START HERE

up from my family that I had to break was the need to go out to dinner every Sunday after church. Originally, I didn't think anything of it. It was a normal part of my routine. However, when I sat down and looked at the numbers, I found that it accounted for a great deal of our food expenses.

TRENDS influence spending when the spending occurs as a result of societal expectations or happens as a result of pressure to follow the crowd. The buzz around trends only exists for a short while. Unfortunately, that's just enough time to cause us to impulsively spend money.

Take, for instance, Hallmark holidays. How many times have you felt as if you were spending money non-stop due to the demand to buy gifts for events like Valentine's Day, Mother's Day, Father's Day, and even Taco Tuesday? When you lump those in with birthdays, anniversaries, and graduations, it adds up to be more than you bargained for.

The feeling of being pressured to spend money also occurs when something big in society happens and everyone is scrambling to be a part of it. Take an iPhone launch for example. All of a sudden, the phone you purchased the previous year doesn't seem to work as well and you are looking for any reason possible to justify an upgrade. Do you see how trend spending can wreak havoc on your finances? The frenzy is a marketing ploy that many fall for.

TRIGGERS influence spending. They can be reactions to a person, environment, emotion, or something as simple as a scent. Trigger spending is the most detrimental form of nonessential spending. Unlike trend spending, trigger spending is done to satisfy a feeling. We all know how powerful feelings can be.

Have you ever had a bad day and felt the need to go shopping as a pick-me-up? Or maybe you went to browse and a store associate made you feel as if you had no business being in that particular store? Then, instead of window shopping, you purchase something to prove a point. What about when you're hanging around a specific group of people? Have

HABITS, TRENDS, AND TRIGGERS

you ever gone to hang out with friends at a restaurant and told yourself you weren't going to spend any money, only to order an appetizer to not feel out of place?

The reason trigger spending can be harmful to our finances is that we often keep spending until that feeling is satisfied. The result of this is usually a bad case of buyer's remorse, sometimes immediately or sometimes even years later.

FOMO was my trigger. When I received an email with the words "SALE" in big, bold letters, I had to take part, and I'd bring my friend Carresse along for the ride. Those sale emails would always draw us in, and as a result, we'd walk out with new outfits and more debt. In our heads, shopping for new clothes was a treat for a stressful day in the lab. We often find ourselves reminiscing about our shopping escapades, and Carresse somehow has a memory of me saying, "I can't repeat outfits if I'm going to an event in the same zip code." Mind you, this was before the rise of Instagram. I don't remember ever saying something like this. Still, if I'm being honest, I probably did, using it as an excuse to shop more. Looking back, we can't believe how naive we were to waste so much money on clothing that we didn't need and no longer even own. It's the reason why hindsight is 20/20. We've found ourselves running through lists of other things we could have done with our funds instead of wearing the newest pair of jeans. We could have invested in some Google stock, gotten a head start on paying back our student loans, put money into retirement accounts, or saved it for future endeavors.

Even though we wasted a large amount of money on clothing, looking back, we can appreciate the lesson that we learned from that experience. By understanding the habits, trends, and triggers behind your spending, you can better understand how and why you misuse money. Most importantly, you can incorporate steps to create a balance that will allow you to reach your financial goals.

How Much Should I Be Spending?

Have you ever been about to purchase something and then stopped and asked yourself, "Am I spending too much?" When it comes to spending money, putting limits on just how much you spend is a reliable way of staying on track and sticking to your financial goals. However, at any point in your life, the amount you should be paying each month on specific categories like housing, basic necessities, and transportation is relative.

The 50/20/30 recommendation as a spending breakdown is a pretty standard example of how one should allocate their after-tax income. For this rule, 50% of your spending goes toward essentials, like your home and utilities. 20% of your spending should be allocated to savings and paying down debt, and 30% is put toward discretionary expenditures, such as vacations and entertainment.

Here's the thing: Staying within these ranges can bring about challenges for those who live in higher-cost areas where the cost of living can easily exceed the recommended 50% range just on housing alone. For other people, medical expenses eat up a good chunk of their monthly income. For this reason, budget breakdowns such as these should only

HOW MUCH SHOULD I BE SPENDING?

be viewed as guides, not steadfast rules, for how you should shape their spending. Remember what I said about personal finance being personal?

Here is where that statement holds true.

Before you worry about how exactly you want to divvy up your money, get a handle on what you're spending. One of the most effective ways to do this is to track your spending. Many banks and credit cards offer a free-spending analysis as a perk for being a customer. If you use a tool like that, you also need to remember to include cash purchases, as well as other credit and debit cards. As a result, many people find it more accurate to use a third-party app or to keep their own records through a spreadsheet or a notebook.

To get an accurate view of how much you're spending, challenge yourself to track your spending each week for at least three weeks. You can use an app or keep a journal. This step is an important one, and you don't want to just skip over it. Tracking your daily spending not only reveals your habits, trends, and triggers; it also allows you to categorize purchases as a want or a need. At the end of each week, look over your expenses and make a note of each expense category. At the end of the challenge, you'll learn a lot about yourself. Plus, you will better be able to create spending breakdown percentages.

Remember that this is your personal spending breakdown, so it's okay if you have more than three categories. If it makes things easier, split the essentials category into three by having one for housing, one for food, and the other for utilities. You can do the same with the categories for discretionary spending, savings, and debt ratios. It's essential that your spending breakdowns make sense for you.

START HERE

50-30-20 SPENDING RATIOS

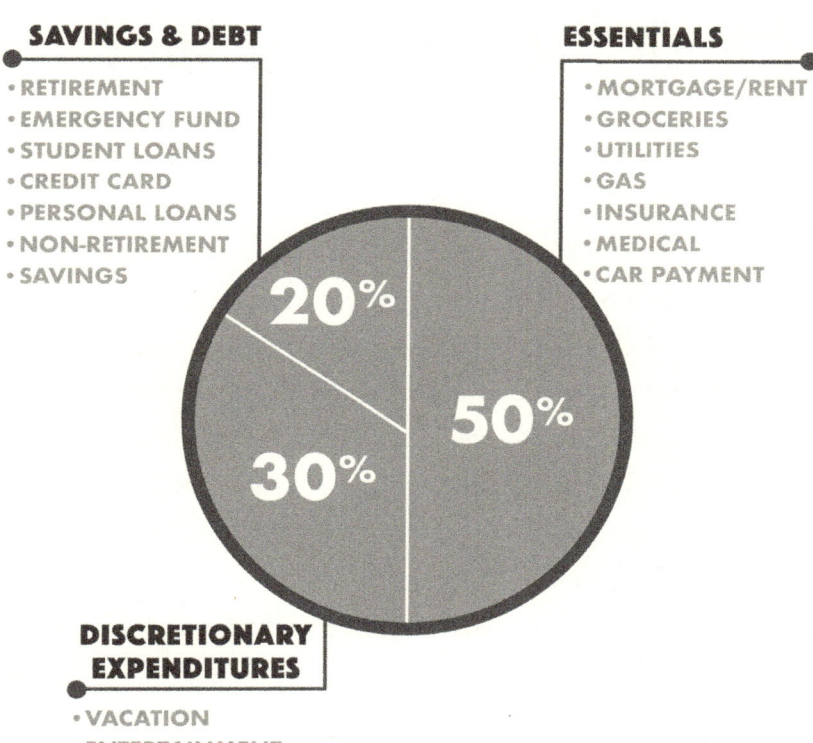

SAVINGS & DEBT
- RETIREMENT
- EMERGENCY FUND
- STUDENT LOANS
- CREDIT CARD
- PERSONAL LOANS
- NON-RETIREMENT
- SAVINGS

ESSENTIALS
- MORTGAGE/RENT
- GROCERIES
- UTILITIES
- GAS
- INSURANCE
- MEDICAL
- CAR PAYMENT

20%
30%
50%

DISCRETIONARY EXPENDITURES
- VACATION
- ENTERTAINMENT
- MEMBERSHIPS
- SELF-CARE
- DINING OUT
- SHOPPING

Cash or Card?
Which One Is Best For You?

Have you ever stopped and thought about what happens when you swipe your debit card? Sure, you pay for your purchase and then receive your goods, but have you ever wondered what's happening on the back end after you swipe? If you answered no, you're not alone. Who has time to think about how their money is coming out of their account when they just scored an awesome deal on something they've been eyeing or they're hangry and want their food?

Emotion is no longer tied to spending when we choose to swipe a debit or credit card, and that's precisely the problem. You don't have to unwad dollar bills or sort through your change purse to find that dime that is camouflaging itself as a penny. You don't have to see the amount of available cash depleting. It's why we're always asking ourselves, "Where did my money go?" By having to physically count out money, you're connecting and parting with your money, prompting you to ask yourself:

CAN I AFFORD IT?

START HERE

By only using cash, you are in control of how much you spend. Plus, you're also more in tune with how and where you're spending. Remember how you felt when you got down to your last twenty- or ten-dollar bill and had to take a moment before going through with your purchase? That intentionality matters. No one likes to see money leaving their hand. They actually do the exact opposite; instead of spending it, they hoard it. Using cash refocuses your intentions and helps put you back in line with what you value.

A excellent method for being more intentional with money is the cash-only method of using money envelopes. While this method creates better money habits, it also takes a lot of self-discipline to make it work. That self-discipline then creates better financial habits. Here's how cash-only spending with money envelopes works. First, start off by creating money envelopes for each spending category where you'll only be using cash.

Some money envelopes might include:
- Groceries
- Dining Out
- Household Stuff
- Entertainment
- Selfcare
- Gas

You can also create envelopes for your personal spending, such as hair, coffee, and the occasional clothing purchase. More than likely, you won't pay your rent or mortgage with cash, so creating an envelope for that category is not needed.

At the beginning of the month (or based on your specific pay schedule), fill each envelope with the amount of cash needed. For instance, if you've planned to spend $300 on groceries this month, either fill your grocery

CASH OR CARD? WHICH ONE IS BEST FOR YOU?

cash envelope with the full $300 for the entire month or split the amount in half, adding $150 every two weeks. Repeat this for all of your envelopes.

Once you have your envelopes set up, the next important step is knowing when to use them. A simple example I love to share is how to use your coffee envelope—or, as we like to call it, your Latte Loot. Whenever you purchase coffee, you pay for it using the money set aside in the designated Latte Loot envelope. Once you run out of money in the envelope, you can no longer purchase coffee until you refill the envelope on your scheduled refill date. The same goes for your gas, groceries, and even entertainment envelopes.

Here's the most common question I hear about money envelopes: "What if I run out of money in the envelope before the month is over?" This is a good question. Most people have an instinct to do something I call "robbing Peter to pay Paul." While you can definitely use money from another envelope to make up a shortfall in another envelope, this behavior may not be ideal. You're actually doing two things: You're going against your outlined budget, and you're completely missing the point of using the money envelope system.

The reason why this cash-only money envelope system is a lesser-used system is that it reprograms your money mindset around spending. For many, it can also be a wake-up call they didn't want. But that wake-up call is so worthwhile. Using the money envelope system does get easier. Like any new habit, the formation takes time. Admittedly, the first couple of months I started using this method to be more intentional in my spending, I found myself in the middle of the month with several empty envelopes. Now, before I spend money, I take the time to seriously think about my purchase. I ask myself questions like, "Do I really want guac on the side at Chipotle?" and "Is a Starbucks run really necessary, or can I make coffee at the office?" Being more deliberate with my money took time to get used to. It also paid off. Since there is physical money leaving your hand with

START HERE

this system, you have more of an attachment to it and want to make sure you're spending it on things you value.

Income is the raw product that your Money Management System manufactures into your financial goals. When you exchange frivolous spending for intentional spending, you're providing a safe path for your money to make it through your system without being detoured. Knowing how you want to use your income is crucial. Do you want to use it to live a life that is just okay or do you want to use it to live the life of your dreams? By realigning your spending with what you truly value and using new methods to help circumvent overspending, you're taking the first steps towards building a successful system.

The Budget/Spending Plan Station

So far on this journey, you've set your financial goals and taken a hard look at how your spending is affecting your income flow into the rest of your Money Management System. It's now time to set up the next piece of your system called the Budget/Spending Plan (BS-P) Station.

The Budget/Spending Plan (BS-P) Station is the most crucial part of your entire system. Think of it as the headquarters for your system where all the stratgeic planning and serious conversations take place. I like to call it the "Regulator." If a major change is going to happen to your Money Management System you can best believe the orders were sent down from here. This BS-P Station is the foundational station that on which the rest of your system is built. Not only does it help to regulate the system; it also assigns a purpose or a job to every single dollar of your income that flows into it. The setup and monthly maintenance of this BS-P Station is critical. Like the "I Love Lucy" example earlier, one mistake can cause issues or backups at other points of your system. Why do you think one of the first questions you're asked when discussing finances is if you have a budget or a spending plan in place? Without it, your system

START HERE

can't operate. You could have all the income in the world, but without the guidance of your budget or spending plan, you'll never be able to reach your financial goals. Remember the outputs that you defined for your Money Management System earlier? Without your B-SP Station in place you'll never see those outputs come to fruition. Using the income that comes into your Money Management System the B-SP station makes sure that all the other stations within the system are supplied with the correct amounts of money so that those outputs can be seen. Using the information provided in the next few chapters you can begin to create a realistic and liveable B-SP station for your Money Management System.

BUDGET/SPENDING PLAN STATION

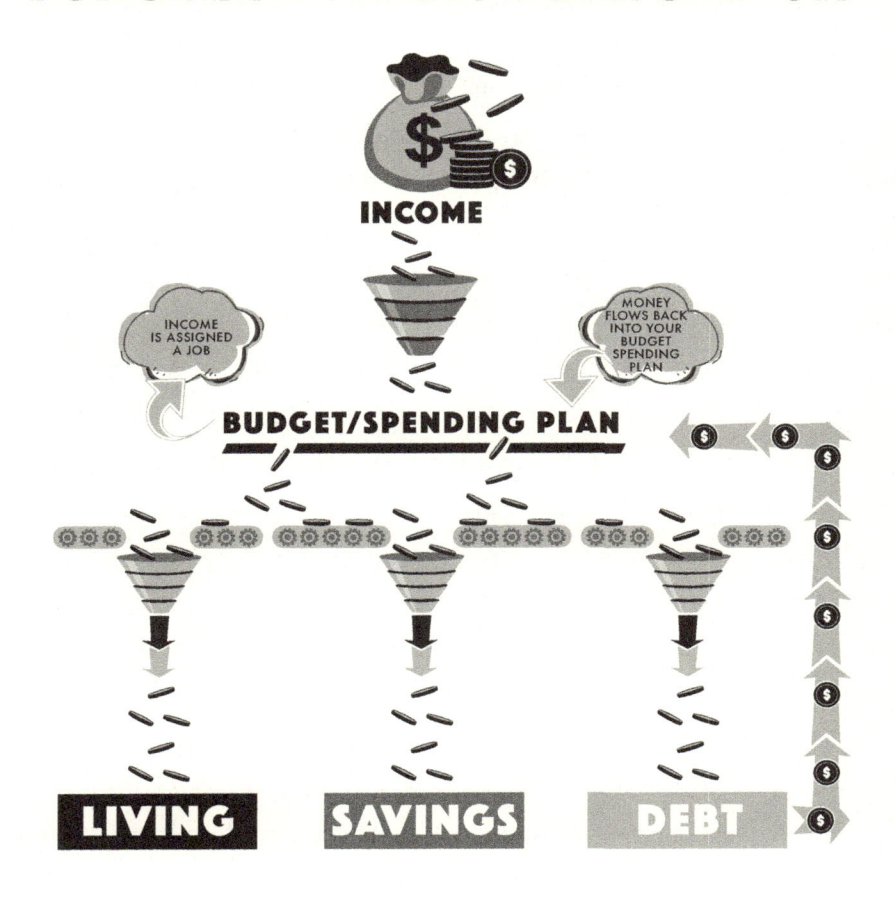

INCOME

INCOME IS ASSIGNED A JOB

MONEY FLOWS BACK INTO YOUR BUDGET SPENDING PLAN

BUDGET/SPENDING PLAN

LIVING   **SAVINGS**   **DEBT**

Your Budget/Spending Plan Is A Box

Boundaries and budgeting go hand in hand. They can either keep things in or keep things out. Another function of a boundary is that it sets restrictions on size or capacity. Your budget or spending plan is made up of an invisible boundary that is set by the size of your income. The larger your income, the more space you have. The smaller your income, the less space you have.

I hate to sound like everyone else, but you need a guide for how you're going to use your income. Many people can quickly feel overwhelmed by the idea of creating a plan for their money. I get it—budgets can feel restricting. Having a budget is preached so much that we unconsciously rebel at the idea because we're tired of hearing about it. There is no getting around having one if you want to make a change with your finances. If you were to put down this book and move on to another one, they'd tell you the same thing. If the "b" word feels like it's a bit too much to handle, you can always interchange the word budget with "spending plan". A spending plan is a written plan for how you plan to *spend* your money for the month. Unlike the word budget, which can sound limiting, a spending

START HERE

plan permits you to spend based on the boundaries of your income.

Here's an easy way to wrap your head around how the B-SP station works. Use this example to help you build out realistic and livable guidelines within your system.

YOUR BUDGET IS A BOX

INCOME

BUDGET/SPENDING PLAN

NON-ESSENTIALS   ESSENTIALS

First, I want you to imagine that your budget or spending plan is a box. The size of that box is based on your income. If you have a substantial monthly income, picture a large box. If your income is modest, imagine a smaller box. No matter the size, this box is rigid. It can't extend beyond its predetermined size unless your income increases. Like all boxes, the space within your box is limited. What you fill the box with and the order in

90

YOUR BUDGET/SPENDING PLAN IS A BOX

which you fill it matter. As you put each item into the box, you'll notice a decrease in the amount of space available. The reduction of space represents the cost of your expenses as they're subtracted from your income. The more expenses you add to the box, the less space is available.

The first step is to make sure the income that flows into your "box" is able to provide room for your Essential Expenses. Your Essential Expenses include everything essential to your survival. Your essentials include your mortgage, groceries, utilities, medical expenses, gas, and the like. Remember that spending tracker that you completed? Use that to help you keep track of the items you put into the box first.

When budgeting for an essential expense like utilities, which have a tendency to fluctuate, a great way to figure out how much you may need every month is to look at the bill from the year prior. If you haven't been in your home for a year, add a minimum of 25% to your estimated utility cost. Summer and winter are seasons where we use the most energy, so you can count on those bills being the highest. If you're enrolled in a budget billing service with your utility company, only budget out the stated amount. One thing you should keep in mind is that if you've used more than the allotted energy amount defined by your budget billing terms at the end of the season or the year, the utility company will charge you for the remaining balance

Once you've covered your Essential Expenses, you should begin to add items needed to cover the Non-Essential Expenses based on their priority in your life. A non-essential expense is any expense that may create comfort in your life, but you don't necessarily need it to survive. These may include your gym membership, cable, weekly hair salon visits, and entertainment. You may find that some categories fall into that gray area of needing it to survive but also being a creature comfort like your car payment or cell phone bill. When in doubt, include these within the non-essential expenses.

START HERE

Add non-essential expenses to your budget based on their importance. For instance, depending on the person, maintaining a weekly brunch date with friends might be more important than having cable. Order them based on your values. Then, keep adding expenses until you run out—either of expenses or space in your box. If you have more room left in your box after all the expenses have been added, congratulate yourself! More space means your income can flow to other areas of your Money Management System. If you've run out of space or money before all the expenses are added to the box, it's a sign that you might be living beyond your means. It's now time to take a good hard look at what's inside. You must decide what stays, what can be reduced, and what should be eliminated.

By following the "Your Budget is a Box" example, you are quickly able to build out the framework for your B-SP Station, as well as the Essential Expenses and Non-Essential Expenses Departments.

Until There's Nothing Left with Zero-Based Budgeting

Having money left after you've built out the framework for your Budget/Spending Plan Station is something to get excited about. It means that you're successfully living below your means! However, it can also lead to mindless or impulse spending, since knowing there is excess can make spending very tempting. When creating your budget or spending plan, the ultimate goal is to make sure that every single cent of your income has a purpose. You're tying your money to your financial goals. This method is also known as Zero-Based Budgeting.

During an Aimlessly Broke Detox session with a client, I challenged her to find a job for the $500+ she had left after she created her spending plan. She admitted that she had trouble with this because having that cushion of money available made her feel safe. To get past this, I had her revisit some of the financial outputs she desired from her Money Management System. By doing this, she was able to get past the fear of losing that perceived safety net. She now knew that the money was still there; it was simply hard at work in another place in the system. She was actually able to cross two things off her list immediately! With every cent

START HERE

of her income being assigned a specific purpose, she was able to be more deliberate about how she utilized her money. She was also able to create a strategic savings plan that would help her fund short-term and long-term goals.

Remember that sometimes your money has to venture to other places in order to maximize its earning potential. By building out your budget or spending plan more precisely, you're creating a life that allows you to have options to live, save, and spend.

Trim The Fat

It's possible that your B-SP doesn't allow you to meet the financial goals you've set due to a shortage of money leftover. If you find yourself in this situation, your next step is to now go through your budget and "trim the fat." Trimming the fat isn't going to be easy. This is where you have to remember that special *why* behind doing this in the first place. You may find that you're going to have to let go of some creature comforts that you love in order for your system to produce its desired output.

Here's how it worked for me. Since we were working as a team, my husband and I both made sacrifices in the name of reaching our financial goals. I cut out items in the Non-Essential Expenses Department like nail salon visits and switched to a hairstyle that would give me more wear time in between salon visits. I even switched to a capsule wardrobe (which turned out to be one of the best decisions I ever made) to decrease spending money on clothes. My husband made the ultimate sacrifice when we agreed to a basic cable package, meaning he lost ESPN during football season. We also gave up going to sit-down restaurants. While these things were difficult in the moment, we knew they were only temporary. Reaching our

START HERE

financial goals was way more important to us. We knew we just needed to live with these sacrifices long enough to build up substantial savings and pay down the debt we'd amassed. We looked at it as a "means to an end."

Here's how you can go about trimming the fat when it comes to your own expenses. First, determine your non-negotiables. A non-negotiable is a category within your budget that you aren't willing to give up. Because this particular item has been defined as a non-negotiable, it can not be included in discussions about cutting or reducing expenses. Though having a non-negotiable item within your budget may seem counterproductive, studies have shown that people are more likely to stick with a plan if it contains an allowance for a small joy or treats. If someone's health is essential to them, they may choose their gym membership as a non-negotiable. If self-care is important, bi-weekly hair or nail appointments may be considered a non-negotiable category. Again, base this on what is going to work best for you.

Next, go through your Essential and Non-Essential Expense Departments and pinpoint the categories where you can reduce your spending.

Ask yourself the following questions:
- Will doing a weekly or monthly meal plan help me save money on groceries?
- Do we need the most expensive cable package?
- Do we need to go out to eat 3x a week?
- Do I need to stop for coffee every single day?
- Is this really the best rate we can get on car insurance?
- How many wears can I get out of these hair extensions?
- Do I need to shop at a premium grocery store?

Lastly, look for expenses within your budget that you would be willing

TRIM THE FAT

to completely cut out either until you're able to reach your financial goals or altogether. You've just trimmed the fat!

The Cost of Cohabitation

My husband and I moved in together right before we got married and quickly found that the 50/50 split when it came to paying bills wasn't going to work for us. Back then, he made significantly more than me. After paying my half, I was left with absolutely nothing to cover non-household bills and other living expenses. On the other hand, he had enough to live it up. To solve this issue, we decided to use a method described by Suze Orman in her book *Young, Fabulous, and Broke*[10], where each couple pays a percentage based on how much they earn. The method is pretty simple:

Step 1: Tally up your combined monthly living expenses.
Step 2: Calculate the total of your combined monthly take-home pay.
Step 3: Divide your expenses by your take-home pay to figure out the percentage
that each of you pays.
Step 4: Multiply the percentage by your take-home pay. This will give you the amount of money each of you pay towards your monthly living expenses.

THE COST OF CO-HABITATING

Example:
Step 1: Monthly living expenses: $3500
Step 2: Your take-home: $2000
   Partner take-home: $4000
   Total= $6000
Step 3: 3500/6000= 0.5833 or 58.3%
Step 4: You (0.583)($2000) = $1166
   Your Partner (0.583)($4000)= $2332

By using this formula, each of you can contribute fairly based on how much you earn while alleviating the financial strain of paying 50/50. This is also a great time to discuss your future and your financial goals as they relate to the relationship. Getting on the same page sooner with your finances alleviates a lot of unforseen headaches that can arise in the future.

After we were married, my husband and I still found ourselves having serious money conversations that should have been discussed before we stood in front of friends and family and said those two big words. Cohabitating, whether you are married or in a serious relationship, doesn't get any easier if you keep putting off conversations about money. It's easy to assume that the other person is "taking care of it." But it's also easy for them to believe the same about you. One of the biggest money conversations my husband and I had was about choosing to combine incomes. I am well aware that this is a controversial topic, and neither one of us grew up with this being the standard action in our family. As I became more familiar with our finances, I knew that by combing our incomes, we'd be able to do a lot more when it came to reaching our financial goals. Combining our incomes allowed us to go a lot further faster because we saw just how much we were working with as a team instead of individuals.

What If I Don't Make Enough?

There will be several times where you find yourself questioning your abilities. You'll wonder if you can actually do the things that you've set out to do with your finances. I remember when I was a new college graduate, and I'd just landed my first job at Charles River Laboratories in Maryland. I was so excited about the new opportunity, but I was also scared out of my mind. I was reluctant to take the job because I would only be making $14.25 per hour. This hourly rate equated to about $2280 a month before taxes and only $1610 after taxes and insurance. When I did the math, I realized that after paying my rent, utilities, and other bills, I would only have around $100 remaining each month. As a 21-year-old, I couldn't wrap my head around surviving on only $100 a month. How was I supposed to get my hair done? What about going out to eat? What about being able to shop? How in the world was I supposed to make it? The draft budget I'd created was super strict and didn't allow room for error. I remember taking these concerns to my mother and explaining my situation to her. What I remember most from this conversation is her response: "All your bills are paid, and you have a job. You'll make it work." I'm sure she probably

WHAT IF I DON'T MAKE ENOUGH

said a lot about it being my first real job, how you have to make sacrifices, and this is precisely what being a grown-up is all about, too. Still, the big thing I took away from the conversation was, "You'll make it work." That's exactly what I did.

My first week living in Maryland, I found a second job at an Express in a mall a couple of minutes from my house. I worked my full-time job Monday through Friday from 7 am until 3:30 pm. Then, I came home and worked my second job from 5:30 pm until close as many days a week as I could. I ate Ramen noodles, and I used coupons at McDonald's so that my Big Mac would only be $1. I would sleep, work, eat, and repeat. Five months later when my job situation changed, I was able to start traveling, thus bringing in more income. I made it work.

I don't share the story above to brag about how hardcore I was. Because let's be honest here, there are families who make less than I did per hour who are doing what they can to make ends meet. They are the real MVP's. I share it to show that sometimes you have to choose to win. I could have resigned myself to just doing the best that I could with that remaining $100. Instead, I chose to do what was necessary for me to stay afloat until my job situation changed. At that time, I didn't have the best money planning skills. Nonetheless, by writing down what I had coming in and what was going out, I knew how much extra money I needed each month to be able to live off the starting salary my job was providing while also paying back my student loan, credit card bills, and other expenses that would have otherwise put me in the red. The most important thing I kept at the forefront of my mind was that working at my part-time job and living on such a strict budget wasn't going to be my life forever. It was a means to an end. A Band-Aid of sorts that allowed me to give my finances a chance to heal.

As you begin to build the Budget/Spending Plan Station of your Money Management System, don't get caught up in numbers. Focus more

START HERE

on what the numbers are telling you. Do you have enough income or do you need to seek additional work to close the deficit? Use the list below to ensure that you're meeting all the requirements of your Essential Expense Department and Non-Essential Expense Department. While this is not an exhaustive list of budgeting categories it can help you get started

HOME

- Rent/Mortgage
- Electricty/Gas
- Gas (Auto)
- Cable/Internet
- Water
- Cell Phone
- Home Phone
- Laundry
- Trash Service
- Household Supplies

INSURANCE

- Car Insurance
- Life Insurance
- Homeowners Insurance
- Renters Insurance
- Pet Insurance

MISCELLANEOUS

- Giving
- Sinking Funds
- Fun Money
- Car Repair
- Home Repair

FOOD

- Groceries
- Dining Out
- Coffee
- Take-out

ENTERTAINMENT

- Movies
- Concerts
- Family Fun
- Hobbies

LIFESTYLE

- Tithes
- Child Care
- Gym Membership
- Subscription Service
- Hair
- Nails
- Travel
- Clothing
- Medicine
- Pet Care
- Property Taxes
- Child Support
- Investments/Retirement

DEBT

- Student Loan
- Car Loan
- Credit Cards
- Personal Loan
- Medical Debt
- IRS Debt

How To Have a Successful Money Meeting

Money meetings are meetings where you (and your partner, if you have one!) sit down to outline the finances for the month while creating a new B-SP. You don't have to be dating or married to have a money meeting. Have a money meeting with yourself. Pour a glass of your favorite drink, put on your favorite song, and crunch those numbers! Make it a ritual, something that you do on a set schedule every month.

If you aren't meeting solo, find ways to make the meeting enjoyable for everyone involved. That drink and that song still work, but you can do more, too! You can do this by sharing an article that you read that may have inspired you or doing a fun activity that shows the progress of your journey.

During a money meeting, make a list of what's coming in along with what's going out. You talk things out and go over goals and values, and you also spend time reflecting on what your life will look like on the other side of your debt. Typically, money meetings are held at the end of the month, allowing you enough time to prepare before the next month's bills start to roll in. Most money meetings range from five minutes to an

START HERE

hour, depending on what needs to be discussed concerning the household finances. The further along you are with your financial journey, and the more experienced you are with writing out your B-SP, the shorter your meetings will be. For my husband and me, our money meetings usually last between five to ten minutes unless something is changing in the upcoming month.

If you're currently doing this journey solo, your money meeting should consist of going over your numbers and spending some time reflecting on your progress and feelings from the last thirty days. When I first attempted to get my financial life together, I wrote a lot of my feelings and reflections in a journal. As times became more difficult and I wanted to quit, I found motivation in revisiting older entries in that journal. Seeing the positive changes to my mindset, growth of saving accounts, and decline of debt pushed me to keep going.

As you review the month, think about whether or not this was a month you want to repeat. Can you see yourself duplicating it in terms of the amount of work you put in to reach the goals you set? Was there anything about the month that you enjoyed or didn't enjoy? If so, what steps can you take to make those moments a more permanent part of your Money Management System or remove them all together? Even though you're going about this alone in terms of making the payments, you don't have to do the entire journey by yourself. Check-in with family, friends, or your accountability partner to let them know how they can support you on your journey.

If you're not on this money journey solo, that can bring its own set of challenges. Having a conversation about money as a family can be hard. Especially if it's a subject that's not often broached in normal conversation or you've had to struggle to get to the point where you're even having a meeting. Money meetings can be awkward, and many people feel that whenever the topic of finances is brought up, their guard has to go up

HOW TO HAVE A SUCCESSFUL MONEY MEETING

as well. They are easily annoyed and irritated. This type of response is a natural reaction that will go away with time.

When having a money meeting, there are basics that all parties involved must keep in mind. To walk away with next month's plan completed and your feelings still intact, I've found that using four foundational leadership behaviors outlined in *Project Management for the Unofficial Project Managers*[11] are the perfect guides to keep your meetings running smoothly.

The four foundational leadership behaviors are:
Demonstrate respect.
Listen first.
Clarify expectations.
Practice accountability.

These parameters are the working basis of many kinds of conversations. In fact, they're foundational for relationships in general. Let's explore how they relate to money meetings in particular.

DEMONSTRATE RESPECT: As I mentioned previously, finances are a sensitive subject. It takes a lot of courage for someone to admit where they've gone wrong financially, and the last thing they want is to feel ridiculed for their bad choices. If you've made it far enough to have a money meeting, then the financial mistakes of the past should be forgiven. Move forward together with a clean slate. During a money meeting, one of the most important things to do is to demonstrate respect towards the other person. If you go into your meeting with an open mind and willingness to treat your partner the way you want to be treated, the meeting will go a lot smoother. Adopt the mantra that communication is key and that there are no stupid questions. By doing this, you allow your partner to feel at ease sharing their feelings.

START HERE

Understandably, the topic of finances may cause some people to become a bit emotional. They may speak more emphatically or with a raised voice. This whole thing may be new or even a bit scary to them. Most of the time, when we make a B-SP, we realize that some drastic things need to take place, like cutting out spending or even reducing the cable package during football season. Don't let their actions affect you.

You can also demonstrate respect by being prepared. Don't go into the meeting without having your numbers ready. Having a list of due dates and amounts owed can shorten the length of a money meeting significantly. If there is a change you'd like to bring up, make sure you've done your research so that you can adequately present how that change would be beneficial to the Money Management System. Being prepared not only shows your partner that you're serious; it also shows them that you respect their time and their feelings.

LISTEN FIRST: A big part of demonstrating respect is knowing how to listen. It can be tempting to dominate the conversation, especially if you've been pouring over personal finance topics and you find that it's something you're passionate about. Remember that this is a team effort. Even if your partner doesn't seem that enthusiastic, what they have to say is just as important as what you have to say. When you fail to listen first, you automatically disregard rule number one, which is to demonstrate respect. Do you see how the two are tied together?

While listening, make sure that you are paying attention to what your partner is saying. If they're voicing concern for a budget category, listen to why they may feel that way, especially if it's a category that primarily affects them. Often when I'm having a conversation, I take notes. That way, I won't forget what's being said as I listen to my husband's concerns. When it's my turn to talk, I can peek at my notes to address key points that he brought up. By listening, you may even find that an idea they brought up would work brilliantly, thus shaving off even more time from your money meeting.

CLARIFY EXPECTATIONS: After making your B-SP, the next crucial thing is to stick to it. Before you close the meeting, you must be sure both of you are on the same page. Clarifying your expectations for the month allows both parties to understand their roles going forward. Address the specific things you want to achieve and the overall goals you want to accomplish with this particular plan in place. One specific expectation could be that you both consistently update the B-SP, keeping each other informed on spending in specific categories. You can easily do this by updating a shared budgeting app. Other overall expectations could also be something like staying within budget for the month or putting an extra $250 in your emergency fund.

PRACTICE ACCOUNTABILITY: When these expectations are clarified, it's up to all parties involved to be sure that they are adhering to them. By practicing accountability, you inspire others to want to do their best as well. You have to lead by example. There's nothing worse than someone who talks a good game, but can never back it up. Some people hate budgets so much that they're looking for any excuse not to do one. If they see you sidestepping or dropping your end of the deal, they're more likely to stop working the plan, too.

Indeed, no one likes to be micromanaged. You must demonstrate respect by trusting your partner to follow through. But what do you do if they don't follow through with the agreed-upon plan? You may find yourself angry and upset because you feel like all your hard work has been derailed. That's understandable. But now it's more important than ever to turn back to the first three rules of Demonstrating Respect, Listening First, and Clarifying Expectations.

When speaking about why things went astray, be mindful that your reaction could make this conversation head in one of two directions: positive or negative. Be respectful of your tone and your approach. Listen

START HERE

to what your partner is saying. Maybe there is an area they are struggling with when it comes to budgeting. Remember, not everyone can stick to a new plan immediately; it's a learned behavior. Once you've heard them out, go back and clarify the expectations for the B-SP. Why do you have one? What was the overall goal? What are your household goals?

It's also important to remember that you might make budgeting missteps from time to time. Accountability also means transparency. I'm not talking about the "I left the top off the toothpaste again" type of openness. I'm talking about the "OMG they might kill me if I tell them this" kind of transparency. You have to be willing to come clean with your mistakes. Covering up the truth will do more harm than good. In fact, covering up the truth may be what got you here in the first place. If you and your partner are making the same error, this may be an area to spend time together troubleshooting.

By practicing the four rules above—demonstrating respect, listening first, clarifying expectations, and practicing accountability—you can have a successful money meeting. The more money meetings you have, the easier they become. Don't let the first few discourage you if they don't get exactly as planned.

Mastering your B-SP is a healthy financial habit that you develop over time. Statistically, it takes three months before someone can successfully form a habit. Even then, you'll find that every month won't be perfect. Don't let slip-ups or mistakes discourage you. We've been living on a monthly B-SP for the past four years, and there are still some months where things slide through the cracks, or one of us forgets to track an expense. Take the time to reflect on each month and write down things you've learned that will help you in the upcoming months. To make things easier, take advantage of automatic bill pay to help you incorporate more convenience into your system, which results in you saving time. Pin down a time for you to be able to focus and create a new B-SP at least a week

HOW TO HAVE A SUCCESSFUL MONEY MEETING

before the start of each month to accommodate any changes in income or new expenses that may arise.

The Savings Station

Call me biased, but the Saving Station is probably my favorite part of the Money Management System. Of course, seeing the income come in is nice, and being organized with my B-SP makes life a lot easier. Still, my Saving Station allows me to see all the fruits of my labor and those things I've been daydreaming about come to life. In short, it reveals progress. Who doesn't get excited about progress?

Two sections make up the savings segment of your Money Management System—the first being your Retirement department and the second being your Non-Retirement department. The major difference between the two is that your Retirement department is preparing you for life after retirement, so that you can live comfortably. Your Non-Retirement department is doing an assortment of things before you retire. It prepares you for expected and unexpected expenses that happen throughout life. It also makes sure that you have money set aside to fund dreams like owning a home and doing other things you love.

But how does money get there? The income that flows into your Money Management System is given an job inside of your BS-P Station

THE SAVINGS STATION

to flow to specific parts of the Savings Station. As you build your Money Management System, you'll be using a variety of savings vehicles. These vehicles will either work towards funding short-term, mid-term, or long-term savings goals within your Savings Station. Once this station is fully functional, you'll begin to see an almost immediate change in your overall financial picture. Additionally, you will also reap the emotional benefits of knowing your goals are beginning to materialize.

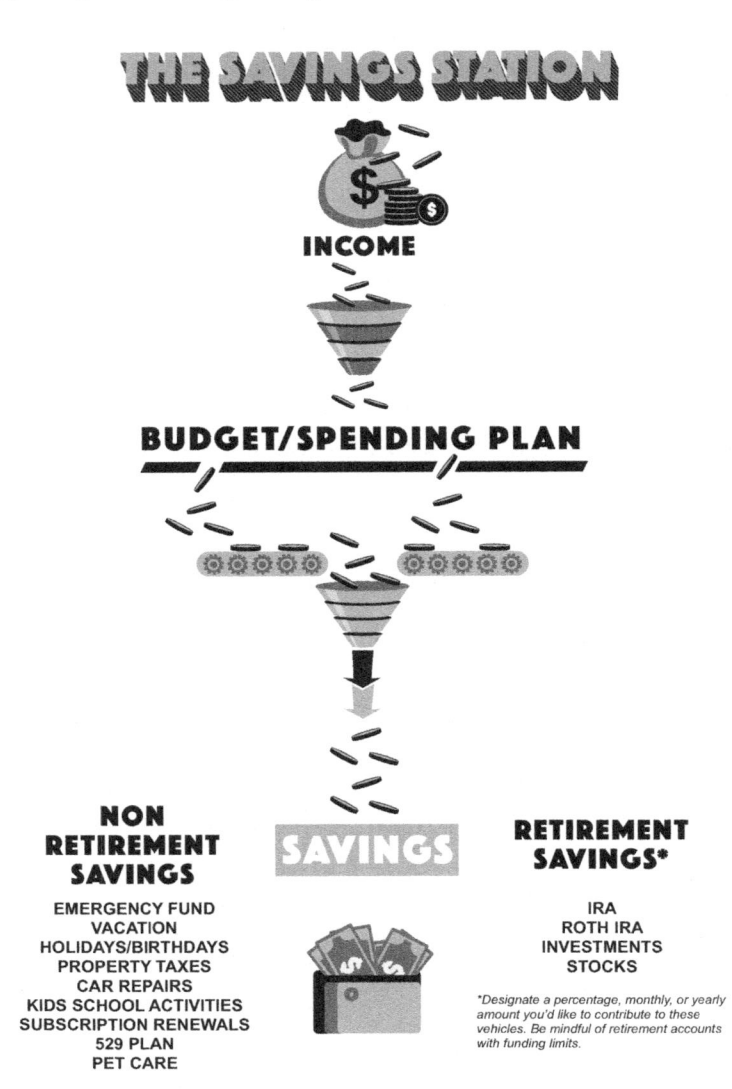

THE SAVINGS STATION

INCOME

BUDGET/SPENDING PLAN

SAVINGS

NON RETIREMENT SAVINGS
EMERGENCY FUND
VACATION
HOLIDAYS/BIRTHDAYS
PROPERTY TAXES
CAR REPAIRS
KIDS SCHOOL ACTIVITIES
SUBSCRIPTION RENEWALS
529 PLAN
PET CARE

RETIREMENT SAVINGS*
IRA
ROTH IRA
INVESTMENTS
STOCKS

*Designate a percentage, monthly, or yearly amount you'd like to contribute to these vehicles. Be mindful of retirement accounts with funding limits.

Savings Accounts Save Lives

Have you ever asked yourself why you should be saving money? Probably not. More than likely, the act of saving money was probably a default behavior passed down from other family members. Or it may have been something that you were deliberately taught. Either way, if you don't take away anything else from this section, just know that not saving money isn't an option.

Ultimately, there are three reasons why we save:
- To have money in case of emergencies,
- To be able to fund future expected expenses, whether they are small or large, and
- To have money for retirement.

Growing up, my Grandma Dot would always tell me to make sure I always "put a little something to the side" whenever I was paid. Now that I'm older, I realize what she was trying to teach me was that I needed to make saving money a habit. In some cases, habits can be detrimental,

SAVINGS ACCOUNTS SAVE LIVES

kind of like the practice of sucking your finger to help you feel calm when you were a kid. For most of us finger suckers, we know what it did to our teeth over time. My grandmother would always chide me about my finger sucking. She hated it and wanted me to stop, but I couldn't. It was something I just "had" to do in order for there to be normalcy in my pretty much "normal" life. What if we developed an obsession with saving money that was just as strong as other habits we have trouble breaking?

When it comes to saving money, this is an area in finances where many people find themselves falling short. While we may have good intentions to save, for some reason, we just can't seem to make it happen. When I was younger, I never took saving seriously. Like a lousy job, my savings account had a terrible turnover rate. The money would go in, and then quickly come right back out. I always "needed" it for something else. It never had a chance to get comfortable, set up shop, and go to work for me. When those situations came about where I seriously needed the money, I found myself sadly without two nickels to rub together.

I know I'm not alone. I'm pretty sure you can share stories about how instead of using your savings account to save money, it took on other unintended roles. To be fair, it's not solely your fault that you picked up these habits. Banks make it easy for us to look at our savings account as a stand-in for our checking accounts. These accounts can take on the role of a revolving door. How quickly did you sign up to have your checking linked to your savings account? The selling point behind this was that in instances where your checking account is overdrawn, the money could come out of your savings account to avoid a late fee. This safety unknowingly gives people permission to overspend, knowing that their savings would be there to cover any overdrafts.

Society tempts us. Banks tempt us. Make no mistake about it—saving is hard work. It takes will power, but it's worth it. Seeing money sitting in your account and telling yourself you can't touch it is like putting a perfectly grilled ribeye steak in front of a dog, saying "leave it," and then walking away. How long do you think that ribeye will sit there before that dog walks away with a full belly? The temptation is just too much! Whenever a client confesses that they can't stop dipping into their savings, I always ask them this one question:

What good is your savings account if it can't save you?

I had to ask myself this very question when we got serious about living Broke on Purpose. What good was our savings account if it didn't have enough money in it to save us from even small emergencies? There were too many instances that we found ourselves without the money to cover things that we should have been easily able to cover. We were hit with a wakeup call as new homeowners when we had to borrow money from a relative to put a new sump pump in our basement. We realized that we didn't even have $1600 in our savings account to cover the cost. Imagine being on cloud nine from buying a home and being hit with the sobering realization that you can't afford the upkeep of your new home?

How Much Should I Have In My Emergency Fund?

Here's the reality of the situation: Because we hadn't made saving a habit or a top priority, we weren't prepared. We didn't have savings to save us, not even in an emergency. We were in desperate need of an emergency fund, which is a savings account solely dedicated to having our backs in times of need. Emergencies are going to happen. They are a natural and often unavoidable part of life. What I've learned on this journey is that our emergency fund makes the difference between an emergency being categorized as an unpleasant situation or an all-out crisis.

Studies have shown that Americans aren't saving money. Most Americans (63%) may not have enough money in savings to cover an unexpected $500 car repair or a $1,000 hospital emergency room visit.[132] Emergency funds are an essential part of any financial plan, and they are one part of your Non-Retirement Savings. An easy way to wrap your mind around an emergency fund is to think of it as a security blanket or a spare tire you keep in your trunk. It's there when you need it. I want you to think about all the times in your life where an emergency fund would have come in handy. Now ask yourself, "If an emergency were to

START HERE

arise today, would you be able to handle it?"

The amount that you should keep in your emergency fund is going to vary from household to household. Typically, amounts between $500-$1000 are suggested for people just starting out, as well as those who are actively paying off debt. The response that I give to all of my coaching clients is to have enough money in your emergency fund that lets you sleep soundly at night. To come up with that number, consider your family size and your overall responsibilities.

Let's keep it real here. $1000 doesn't go as far as it used to. Remember when the government shut down in 2018 for almost a month? 80,000 people went without pay.[13] How fast do you think they went through their $1000 emergency funds—that is if they had one? People found themselves in situations where they had to take out loans, secure other jobs, or sell items to make ends meet. While the government workers were eventually paid, government contractors weren't so lucky. As a result of the shutdown, lives were changed forever.

One of my good friends described $1000 as being the new $20, and she's right. We have to be mindful of the fact that money doesn't go as far as it used to. If you have a family with family-sized responsibilities, you can wipe out that amount in an instant. Instead of limiting your emergency fund to $500 or $1000, use that as a starting point. Then, consistently add to it, building it up to an amount that makes you feel more comfortable. Remember, saving money can also be done while working to achieve other financial goals.

It's essential to remember that emergency funds should be used only in, well... the case of an emergency. An emergency fund is there to have your back, but you don't want to put it in play unnecessarily.

If you're wondering what constitutes an emergency, ask yourself the following:

HOW MUCH SHOULD I HAVE IN MY EMERGENCY FUND?

1. Can I live without it, or is it a necessity?
2. Is it unexpected?

To make sure you aren't just grazing over the questions, let's explore what you should consider in both instances. By taking a deeper dive, you will be more likely to conserve your emergency fund. That's the point. Keep it stocked so that it remains until a real emergency.

Can I live without it or is it a necessity? When faced with an unexpected emergency, take some time to think about the situation before impulsively reacting. If you're dealing with unexpected car repairs that will keep you from getting back and forth to work, then you would consider the situation an emergency. However, your TV going out does not fall into the same category.

Is it unexpected? You may think this question is silly, but you'd be surprised at how many times people view expected bills as emergencies. Do not use your emergency fund to cover items that can and should be a working part of your B-SP. If your car insurance is due every six months, work the payments into your monthly plan and set it aside.

Let's test out a scenario. Your favorite artist randomly and unexpectedly decides to go on tour. Should your emergency fund foot the bill for concert tickets? Buying concert tickets does not constitute the proper use of your emergency fund. It's true that the concert may be unexpected. Plus, having the money available may be tempting. But go back to the first question. Can you live without it or is it a necessity? Since you can survive, it's not a necessity.

There are some exceptions to this rule. One alternative is when dealing with a bill that is larger than what you anticipated due to fluctuations in rates (we see this a lot with utility bills). In that case, what you've budgeted may not be enough to cover the amount. Here, dipping into your emergency fund to make up the difference so that you do not incur a late fee is a valid use. Still, do all that you can to keep your emergency fund intact, so you're prepared if and when disaster actually does strike.

My Emergency Fund Had My Back

If you need some extra convincing about how important it is to have your Saving Station up and running, let me share with you how the Emergency Fund in my Non-Retirement Savings Station had my back.

After graduating with my Ph.D., I stayed on to finish up some work in the lab. Because I'd graduated, I could no longer be paid as a student and had to be paid as a tech or a postdoc, which meant an increase of around $20,000 per year. With June already underway, I'd been informed that I would see the difference in pay on my July paycheck. Without the increase in June, retro pay was supposed to be added to my pay in July.

At the end of July, I received my monthly paycheck and immediately noticed that something was wrong. My gross pay was over $7000, and I netted ~$5300. My normal gross pay should have been around $3950 for the month. This suspicion was confirmed when I received an email from someone in administration telling me that I'd been overpaid. Instead of receiving retro pay for the difference I was supposed to receive in June, they'd inadvertently paid me another full paycheck. In a nutshell, I was paid twice. It was a mistake that I completely understood, and I asked them to let me know how much I should return.

Shortly, I received an email asking me to return $2197, which equates to the student salary I received in June. There was only one problem: I couldn't do that. If I did give them back the $2197, then I would be the one losing money, not them.

Here's why:

When I was overpaid (or double paid, whatever you want to call it), it placed me in a higher tax bracket.

The increase in pay caused an increase in the amount of taxes that were siphoned out of my paycheck.

It was unfair for me to lose money for a mistake that they made.

Upon explaining the reasons why I could not give them that amount, I was told that they weren't liable for the taxes and that I would possibly get them back next year when I filed my income taxes. I was told this by two different people! I was even told, "We don't refund taxes, so I don't know what you want us to do."

Here's the main problem: No one cared that the mistake occurred on their end; they just wanted their money. I wanted to give them their money, but I also wanted it to be fair.

After going back and forth with payroll, I was finally fed up with the whole thing, so I just asked them to take the money back. It's not every day that someone has the guts to ask payroll to take their money back, so the request caught them off guard. I requested a payroll reversal. This would allow them to reissue me a paycheck for the correct amount. Since the payment was made via direct deposit, they had the capability to do so.

This is how the conversation went.

Them: You know that means you have to give back everything.

MY EMERGENCY FUND HAD MY BACK

Me: I'm aware.
Them: It comes out immediately.
Me: Okay.
Them: Can you cover it? You won't get repaid until the next Friday.
Me: Yes, that's what emergency funds are for.

A few days went by before the Payroll Office finally did the reversal, and I was issued two separate checks. One check was for my normal pay, and one was for my retro pay. The total of those two after taxes equaled more than what I would have left with had I just given back the $2197 without a fight.

Certainly, this situation is unusual and highly specific. The chances of you finding yourself in the same position are slim. The chances of you finding yourself in a similar position, though, are much more likely. If you haven't already, you will quickly learn no one cares more about your money than you do.

Here are four things I learned from this situation that I think everyone can apply to their own finances.

Lesson One: In this situation, my emergency fund gave me an option. Instead of having to accept their answer and lose money as a result of their error, I was able to transfer money from our emergency fund to cover us while they sorted things out. My emergency fund stepped in and had my back and allowed me to make an unstressed decision.

Lesson Two: Your emergency fund should feel like a comfort. Even though we had enough in our emergency fund to cover this "situation," actually having to use it was a wake-up call. Our amount made me feel uneasy, and I asked myself if what we had was actually enough. I realized that what we had no longer gave me the peace of mind that it used to and that we would need to work towards increasing it.

Lesson Three: Advocate for yourself when no one else will. In this situation, I had two people in two different departments tell me that I was just going to have to deal with the fact that taxes had taken the extra money. They didn't say, "Let's see what we can do" or "Give us time to figure it out." They said, "You owe us this. When can you pay it back?" Understandably, with all of this going on, I was becoming very irritated. Like anyone, I don't like my money to be messed with, but I had to stay calm and collected. I needed my concerns—not my emotions or their perception of me being a "student who didn't know anything"—to be heard. Most people are intimidated when it comes to money conversations. People start throwing out numbers or percentages, and you immediately want to shut down. If you don't understand, go to someone that does, explain the situation, and have them come with you to talk it through. Remember that the best fix isn't always going to be the first one you think of or the cheapest.

Lesson Four: Don't wait for an emergency to start building an emergency fund. We were lucky this time. Had this occurred two years earlier, we would have had to eat the loss or ask one of our parents for money. You should never get so comfortable that you think financial emergencies won't happen.

As we continue to move forward, make sure that saving up for an Emergency Fund is one of your financial roadmap goals. Come up with the total amount and break it down further into an amount you can attend to save monthly.

Where Should I Keep My Money?

Don't put all your eggs in one basket: This is probably one of the most real sayings of all time. If you want to get biblical about it, read Ecclesiastes 11:1-2, which says, *"Send your grain across the seas, and in time, profits will flow back to you. But divide your investments among many places, for you do not know what risks might lie ahead."* If you ask me, it sounds like the Bible is even telling you how important it is to set up your Saving Station. When it comes to saving money, I'm a follower of these principles. My motto now is to always be preparing for a famine while enjoying a feast. You have to start saving now—like right now!—if you want to be prepared for anything!

In my financial empowerment sessions, clients often confess that they struggle with keeping their hands out of their cookie jars. Seeing the savings build-up is just too tempting, and they can't help but find themselves breaking off what they believe to be a small and harmless piece of savings. While we do discuss default behaviors that lead to these actions, I also advise them that where they keep their money is going to be key to their success. Traditional brick and mortar banks may not be the best fit anymore. To reduce the temptation, I advise clients to move any money that does not need to be obtained quickly to a place where it's not easily accessible. Doing this does two things: It reduces the temptation you feel when you see it, and it removes easy access. Think of it like when you have a young child that keeps touching and grabbing on things. What do you do? You move the objects out of reach. Use that same principle with your money if you can't keep your hands off of it.

In today's day and age, you'll find that banks actually offer more incentives for doing all your banking online. It's almost as if they're paying you to not have to deal with you. Online banks that have few or no brick and mortar stores, such as Capital One 360 and Ally, are capitalizing on one big thing—the convenience factor. People want the benefits of an online bank and want to be able to access those benefits wherever they are.

People who are working to curb the habit of dipping into their savings account may find that having non-emergency accounts at an online bank works in their favor. One of the quirks of an online bank is that things don't move as fast as being able to walk into an actual building and withdraw money. If you're using an online bank to hold your savings, you have to initiate a transfer to a checking account to gain access to your money. This transaction can take up to three days if the accounts aren't within the same financial institution. What many find is that this delay actually works in their favor. Due to the delay, they now have time to really think about what they are planning on using that money for and decide if it is actually worth it. Also, because access to that money isn't instantaneous, they're more likely to leave it alone. The perceived hassle of the transfer curtails impulse spending.

Like traditional banks, online banks allow you to fund your accounts easily by establishing automatic transfers, by manually scheduling deposits from your linked checking account, or by setting up deposits via payroll so that money is deposited every time you get paid. You'll also find that

WHERE SHOULD I KEEP MY MONEY?

saving accounts held in online banks may not have required minimums or charge as many fees. One last bonus is that online savings accounts at online banks typically have an APY (annual percentage yield) that is considerably higher than traditional banks. Being able to earn extra money while you save is always great One account I would not recommend keeping in an online bank that you don't have quick, direct access to would be your Emergency Fund. In case of an emergency, you need access to that money quickly and don't have the comfort of time to wait up to 3 days for the transfer to complete. If your Emergency fund is of significant size, keep a small percentage in a separate easy to access savings account so that it is available to you at all times.

Stacking Your Non-Retirement Coins

You probably came up with quite a list of short-term and long-term savings goals as you wrote out your overall financial goals. You likely identified future endeavors, expected expenses, and an emergency fund to cover the unexpected. The money that flows into your Savings Station comes from your B-SP Station. However, the only way the B-SP Station can approve this transaction is if the amounts are part of the monthly plan. Each month, your B-SP needs to know how much of your income should be allocated to specific savings goals from your Non-Retirement and Retirement Savings Departments.

Commingling your money when it comes to saving is never a great idea. Each savings goal you create within your financial plan should have a separate savings account. It sets clear boundaries and allows you to see how much you've saved for a particular objective instead of estimating. I call these separate savings accounts sinking funds. In a regular savings account, money is deposited with the sole purpose of saving. Unlike a regular savings account, a sinking fund is an account that has a specific purpose and goal amount. Instead of having money put aside as a just in case, you're saving for something specific in a sinking fund. For example,

STACKING YOUR NON-RETIREMENT COINS

I have sinking funds to cover the expected cost of car repairs, yearly subscription renewals, vacation, vet bills, phone upgrades, holidays, celebrations, and more. If I anticipate a future expense, I start saving for it immediately. By *sinking* money into a designated savings account each month, you're relieving yourself of the stress that would naturally accompany that expense.

Most of your savings goals found within the Non-Retirement Savings Department will be funded using the sinking fund method. Since you may be funding several saving goals simultaneously, an online bank that allows customers to open online savings accounts with no minimums or fees would be beneficial. I've employed the multiple savings accounts method using online savings accounts for years. Still, I never truly appreciated their true value in terms of ease, organization, and structure until I got into building my Money Management System.

Sinking funds will have others wondering how you're able to afford your lifestyle. People will want to know how you can do all that you do and never worry about how you're going to pay for it. As you've seen with the earlier parts of building your Money Management System, preparation is key. Not only do sinking funds allow you to be prepared for expenses when they arise, they give you permission to spend!

It was only when I decided not to go through with funding a sinking fund that I realized how important they were to my financial well being. The worst time to start saving for an expense is when it's knocking on your door with its hand out. Ever need new tires and not have new tire money? It sucks, doesn't it? I went through this with my laptop. I have had my MacBook Pro since the beginning of 2011. It helped me build two brands and got me through graduate school. While I had thoughts of replacing it, I didn't feel an immediate need because the laptop did everything I needed it to do and did it well. That is until I spilled Ranch dressing on it. Don't ask me how I did it; I'm already embarrassed enough as it is. To make a long story short, our best efforts couldn't save the computer, and I was forced to get a new one. Here's the worst part. I actually started saving up for a new computer at the beginning of the year and then decided I didn't need the savings. So I used that money for something else. So here I was facing this emergency of needing a new MacBook Pro (I'm an Apple girl, sorry), and I didn't have any money earmarked for it. Don't let this be you. Don't wait until you're in the face of an expense to wish you would have prepared for it. Oh, and don't eat around your laptop!

To calculate how much you should put into a sinking fund, use the example below as a guide.

Penny wants to set up a short-term savings goal within her Non-Retirement Savings Station. Her goal is to have $1000 to spend on gifts for Christmas. She plans to start saving on January 1st of the new year and wants to be able to use the money in December, giving her 12 months to save.

Sinking Fund Formula:
Savings Goal/Months to Save = Monthly Saving Amount

$1000/12 = $83.33   Monthly Saving Amount: $83.33

Based on this information, Penny would first add a Christmas category to the B-SP Station of her Money Management System. Doing this will help her account for the amount that needs to flow to her Savings Station monthly and to make sure there is enough income to fund it. She would then either manually deposit or set up automatic transfers of $83.33 to a sinking fund specifically designated for Christmas. By the time she needs the Christmas fund, it will be there for her.

Use the formula above to help you plan out how much you need to fund the short-term, mid-term, or long-term goals within your Non-Retirement Savings Department. Since sinking funds have specific saving amounts, plan out your savings based on your priorities. Determine which goals are important for you to fund immediately and which goals you can start once others are complete. As your emergency fund is the most essential, be sure it is at the top of your list. Don't forget to include the monthly savings amount into your B-SP Station to ensure that there is enough income available to cover the monthly savings goal.

In It For The Long Haul

The Retirement Savings Department of your Money Management System handles all your non-job-related retirement savings. Even though this section is about retirement, I'm not going to go into asset allocation or how conservative or aggressive you should be investing your money. I'm also not going to spend time telling you *where* you should be investing your money. The reason being strategies on saving for retirement are unique and based on the personal side of personal finances. What I am going to tell you is that due to the many nuances that go into retirement savings, it's ideal that you consult with a certified financial planner. They can better assist you with understanding your options and investment strategies as they relate to your financial situation.

Retirement is one of those things that seems like it's always a long way off until you blink your eyes and realize you don't have much time left to build savings for it. Saving for retirement is just as important as putting money into your emergency fund or preparing for upcoming expenses with sinking funds. According to a survey by GoBankingRates, 64% of Americans are expected to retire with less than $10,000 in retirement savings accounts.[14] If there is one concept concerning retirement that you need to know, it is that compounding is your friend. Simply put, compounding is the method by which your earnings and profits go on to earn profits of their own. Think about compounding this way. When you start a family, your children (which are your initial investment) go on to have children of their own, causing your family to grow (this is compounding). As your children's children have children, your family continues to grow, and your children's families continue to grow. Pretty soon, you have this massive family tree to look back to, and it all started with you making that initial investment of having a child! Now imagine that happening with your money, and it can all start with one dollar! Due to the power of compounding, saving for retirement is not something you should put off. Time is your ally here, so the sooner you start, the better.

When I started graduate school in 2008, the school paid me to attend classes and work in the lab. One of the things not included in their package was a sponsored retirement plan. Since I'd had a traditional job before going back to school, I knew how important it was to put at least something into a retirement account. Although I was on a very limited budget, I made sure to put at least $34 into a Roth IRA every month. Luckily for me, the brokerage account I used at the time let me purchase fractional shares of stocks and ETFs (exchange-traded funds). That brokerage company has since been sold to another company, and the perks of buying partial shares is no longer an option. So, I've taken my business elsewhere; however, it's still astonishing to see how much my investment of $34 each month has grown. That investment is going to continue to grow thanks to reinvesting dividends, compounding, and saving early in my 20s.

An article from USAA[15] describes compound interest as being "POWERFUL." I feel they are 100% correct in their description. The article goes on to show that the difference between saving for retirement at 22 years of age with an additional 40 years of savings versus starting at 42 years of age and an additional 20 years of savings. Both scenarios end at the age of 62. They also factor in the same starting amount of $1,000 in retirement savings, an added $100 per month, and an estimated rate of return of 6 percent. The difference amounts to $160,592! Because the 22-year-old has time on their side, they are projected to save $210,106 compared to $49,514 for the 42-year-old.

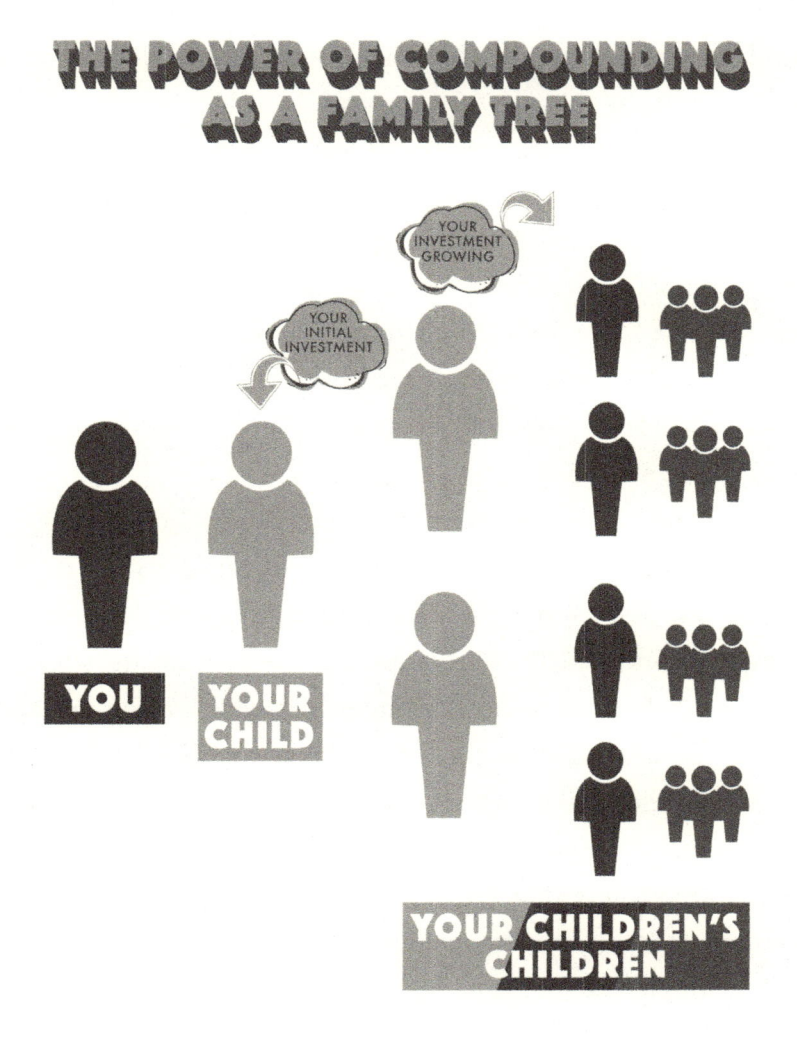

THE POWER OF COMPOUNDING AS A FAMILY TREE

YOUR INITIAL INVESTMENT

YOUR INVESTMENT GROWING

YOU | YOUR CHILD

YOUR CHILDREN'S CHILDREN

IN IT FOR THE LONG HAUL

Understandably, large numbers can be intimidating. Please allow me to break this down in a much more palatable form. Let's say you're starting with an original investment of $1000. That account has an extraordinary rate of return of 10%. At the end of the year, you will have earned an additional $100 on your initial investment. Now, here's where it gets good. If you were to reinvest or leave that money in the account for another year, you make even more money! If the rate stays at 10%, you'll again make $100 on your initial investment plus an extra $10 on the $100 profit you made the year before. Imagine this kind of magic happening in the background for years! Actually, don't imagine it, make it happen! Okay, maybe some might say that a 10% return run is a bit far fetched, but the concept is still very much real. Don't be afraid to let your money multiply!

To get a better picture of how the power of compounding can work for you, estimate your numbers by using a compound interest calculator. Play with the numbers. Start with an initial investment of $100. Then see how much saving $1/day for 40 years at an 8% return will give you. Now change that $1 to $5 a day, which is the cost of lunch or a fancy cup of coffee. Every time I put numbers into a compound interest calculator, I feel giddy at the potential of what a single dollar can do.

Now let me be a little transparent here. Sometimes I read articles that talk about people taking full advantage of funding retirement in their 20's and I get discouraged. Even though I put something into my retirement, it wasn't anywhere near $100 -$250 a month. It makes me question if I'll ever have enough for retirement. I wonder if maybe I'm too late to the game. Then I remember that starting in my 20's has nothing to do with my ability to maximize or make the most out of my retirement savings now. I can't keep looking at the past wishing for a do-over. I have to take hold of the time and opportunity that I have in front of me.

In today's economy, where people are juggling so much financially, retirement savings tend to take a back seat within financial plans. Not being able to put the recommended 10% of your income towards retirement isn't the end of the world. The most important thing is that you save what you can. Should you have the luxury of being able to contribute to a company-sponsored retirement plan, like a 401K, 403b, or Thrift Savings Plan, do not pass up this job-related perk. These plans allow you to save for retirement automatically before you receive your paycheck. They also reduce your overall amount of taxable income, since the money is taken out before taxes. In theory, that means you take home more money. Another benefit of taking advantage of a company-sponsored retirement account is that some will match the amount you contribute up to a certain percentage. Retirement matching is a pretty big deal because it's FREE MONEY! Often a company will match 3% of the first 6% you contribute. If you put $1 into your company-sponsored retirement account, they'll match it by $0.50. Not taking advantage of this match leaves money on the table.

If your job doesn't offer retirement benefits, you can contribute to an Individual Retirement Account, also known as IRA. IRAs come in two main flavors: Traditional and Roth.

Here's a bit more about each type of IRA:

Traditional IRA: This account is tax-deferred. That means you can make tax-deductible contributions based on your income, and your money will grow tax-deferred while it is invested. Because this is a tax-deferred account, taxes will be paid on all money withdrawn after retirement. At age 70 1/2, you are required to take minimum distributions. If you do not meet the deductibility rules, you can still contribute to an IRA. The only difference is that your contributions will not be deductible. You will still, however, be able to grow your income tax-deferred until it is withdrawn at retirement. Those who are self-employed can open a SEP (Simplified Employee Pension), which works like a traditional IRA but has higher contribution limits. Before opening a traditional or SEP IRA, you want to review the eligibility rules and limits. You may also want to speak with a certified financial planner to help you maximize your investments for retirement.

Roth IRA: This type of account is considered tax-exempt since it is funded with after-tax income. You cannot claim tax deductions on a Roth IRA. Unlike a traditional IRA, your withdrawals will be 100% tax-free in retirement. However, there are a few caveats. You have to wait until age 59 ½ to withdraw earnings on your original contribution, and you have to have had the account for at least five years. Unlike a traditional IRA, there are no required minimum distributions. You can choose to use the money upon eligibility or leave it untouched, allowing it to keep growing. One of the perks to having a Roth IRA is that in a pinch, it can act like a backup emergency fund. Because you fund the account with after-tax dollars, you are free to withdraw your original contributions (not the earnings) at any age without incurring taxes or penalties. Anyone can invest into a Roth IRA; for those who exceed income limits, you can invest in a non-deductible IRA and have that account converted to a Roth IRA.

You can open an IRA at the financial institution of your choosing. Like company-sponsored accounts, IRAs have contribution limits. For 2020, the maximum that you can contribute to an IRA is $6000. If you're 50 and over, the catch-up contribution limit is $1000, thus allowing you to save a maximum of $7000. Checking the contribution limits and income limits each year can help you make better savings decisions since the amounts do change from time to time.

When building your Retirement Savings Station, you may choose to invest a certain percentage of your income or a monthly amount in the stock market, or you may choose to fund an IRA or other investment-related plans. Whichever you choose, always make sure that the information is relayed to the B-SP Station so that it doesn't affect the flow of your money elsewhere in your system.

Saving When You Don't Have Anything To Save

We can all agree that saving money is important. It's a safety net that keeps us afloat when the world tries to pull the rug from under us. However, one thing that I've come to realize in my time as a financial empowerment coach is that saving money is a privilege. People on the outside looking in are quick to make assumptions about the way others live. What many fail to realize is that it goes beyond living below your means and taking on extra jobs. According to a 2017 report by CareerBuilder, 80% of Americans live paycheck to paycheck, many working multiple jobs to make ends meet.[16] So, even if someone wanted to save money, there are many factors, including economic constraints, crippling student loan debt, increased costs of living, and stagnant wages, that prevent saving from being an immediate option.

So how does one go about saving up a sufficient emergency fund, putting away money for upcoming expenses when the budget is already tight, or saving for retirement? As simple as it may seem, the answer is to just start. Don't get caught up in the idea of having to save a certain percentage of your income every month. If you can only save $5 a month,

SAVING WHEN YOU DON'T HAVE ANYTHING TO SAVE

make it your goal to save $5 a month. As things in your life begin to change positively, you can slowly increase the amount you're funneling into your Non-Retirement or Retirement Departments of your Money Management System. Saving money isn't about sprinting to the finish line; it's a marathon. No matter if you're walking or running, every step counts toward your savings goal. The earlier you start building your savings, the better off you'll be in the future. A creative way to start a savings account is to ask for account contributions in lieu of gifts during the holidays or ask someone to pay a bill so that money is freed up for you to put into your savings account. No matter how you do it, the practice of saving, even if it's small, is better than the thought of doing it some other day.

Here's a small list of possibilities to get you started:
- Collect found money—loose change you come across—and deposit it monthly.
- Call to see if you can reduce one bill, even by just a few dollars, and save the difference.
- Put any monetary gifts into your savings accounts.
- Sell something you no longer need or use and save the amount you make.

The one place in my home where I found a lot of extra money was inside my closet. While it wasn't sitting there in actual dollar bills, it was present in the form of clothing and shoes I was no longer wearing or things with price tags still on them that I'd purchased. All those "good deals" never saw the light of day unless I opened the closet door. Among the items sold were my coveted pair of Valentino Rockstud pumps. I felt like a bonafide big deal when I first purchased these shoes. I acquired them as a result of trend spending. Everyone in my circle had a pair, so I had to have a pair too. As much as I loved being the owner of these designer

START HERE

shoes, I didn't wear them enough to justify the high cost. By leveraging online consignment shops, like Poshmark and Tradesy, I was able to turn those clothes and shoes into over $3000 of extra cash that we added into our Money Management System. Not only did I walk away with the extra money, but I also had a cleaner closet and a greater appreciation for how I would spend my money on clothing and accessories going forward.

Another great way to make additional money for your savings is to use your talents. Believe it or not, we all possess a skill that can be used to create extra income. You may have a knack for editing/proofreading, graphic design, organizing, sewing, crafting, or even training. If you aren't sure what your talent is, think about the one thing people are always asking you to do for them. What are you the go-to person for? Don't be afraid to get creative and share your talents beyond family and friends.

Ready, Set, Save!

Before moving onto the next section, stop here and take some time to plan out your Non-Retirement and Retirement Saving Departments of your Money Management System.

For your Non-Retirement Department, start by revisiting your goals and listing out expenses that you expect to incur for a full year. These expenses may include car insurance, property taxes, membership dues, or vacation. Use the Sinking Fund formula in the *Stacking Your Non-Retirement Coins* chapter to find out how much to set aside each month to fund your goal. Do the same for unexpected expenses that may arise, like car or home maintenance. Although you expect expenses in these areas to occur, one is never too sure what the money may be spent on. The best practice is to estimate an amount to save that feels comfortable. For instance, because we have two older cars as a household, we set a limit of having $2000 in an online sinking fund for car repairs. We fund that by saving $150 each month. Should something happen to both cars at the same time, this is enough to cover the potential cost of both repairs.

To plan your Retirement Department, decide how much you'd like to save yearly. Then, break it down into a monthly cost that you work into your B-SP Station. Remember to be mindful of investing limits. If you can't meet the limit, don't get discouraged. Every little bit counts. With time and the power of compounding, you will see your money grow. If you have the option, take advantage of job-sponsored retirement plans that could earn you a matching percentage or dollar amount from your company. You also want to pay special attention to your Retirement Station if you don't have access to a company-sponsored retirement account.

Fund the items in your Savings Station based on order of priority. If you're unsure which items to save for first, take a look at your B-SP to see how much income is remaining after the Living Station has been fully funded. Route some or all of that excess to your Savings Station.

Even if you don't feel you're at a place yet where you can actively start saving beyond an emergency fund, knowing what the numbers look like will help you become more clear in your plans moving forward.

The Debt Station

In this section, we'll be covering your Debt Station. The Debt Station is the last station within your Money Management System. However, being last doesn't mean that it's any less important. You may find that this is where most of the money in your B-SP plan is flowing, which makes it one of the most important pieces of your system to put in place. The goal here is to have as little money as possible flowing into this portion of your Money Management System because it would mean you have little to no debt. You don't need to have the other pieces of your Money Management System up and running in order to build your Debt Station. Acknowledging all of your debt and sitting down to come up with a plan for paying it back is a great starting point. With this in place, you can connect the other pieces of your Money Management System to see how well it functions and what needs to be adjusted as a result. Building out our Debt Station allowed us to clearly see how much debt we had, and which debts were doing the most damage. The resulting plan of action also helped us to minimize the amount of time we spent paying things off. Time matters—we all know that time is a currency, just like money.

START HERE

Almost everyone would like to go back to a time in their lives when they didn't have any debt. Those were the good old days. Now that you've amassed a certain amount of debt—be it from student loans, financing a car, taking on a mortgage, or using credit cards—you've probably found that it was a lot easier to get into debt than it is to get out of it. Debt can also be addictive. It's why many look for reasons to go back into debt once they've successfully dug themselves out of it. Take, for example, someone who successfully pays off their car. Instead of being satisfied with a paid-off car and the extra money that's now available to them, they'll instead look for any excuse they can find to justify financing another one. For many, taking on debt provides access, and to keep that access, they'll choose to stay in the same repetitive cycle. However, for many, debt is also the only way to get access and unfortunately is unavoidable.

Truthfully, debt is also a roadblock. It reduces our quality of life and limits our options. Instead of allowing us to get ahead, it holds us back. At least that's how I felt about my debt. It seemed that not a day went by where my debt didn't remind me that I couldn't afford to do the things that I wanted to do. I'll never forget the day I heard the pastor at my church exclaim, "Debt is stealing from your future to pay for your present!" I wanted to get up and run screaming around the pews! He was right. Not only was I paying for my present, but I was also still paying for my past.

It is important to understand that your debt can even keep you from getting a job because employers use that as an indicator of your ability to be responsible. There are many reasons why we get into debt, so I won't get into the whole "good" debt vs. "bad" debt argument, as the reasoning is relative. However, I will say that if your debt causes any amount of undue stress in your life, there is nothing good about it. So why keep it around?

Here's where the added benefits of the planning and organization found within your Money Management System are extremely beneficial. There are many methods one can use to pay down debt, and they all have their pros and cons. However, before choosing one to incorporate into your system, it's important that you are crystal clear on three things:

1. How much you owe,
2. Who you owe it to, and
3. The terms and conditions that go along with that particular debt.

Just having an idea of what you owe won't cut it. As scary as it may be, knowing your numbers is only going to empower you as you move forward. Those precise numbers will help with choosing a debt repayment method that will work best within your Money Management System. Before proceeding, create a list of all your debts, including loans from family and friends. Make sure to include the total balance, interest rates, due dates, promotions, and any late fees. Having this information on hand will help you to weigh the pros and cons of each repayment method and choose the one that works best for your specific situation.

I've said this several times throughout this book, and I'll say it again: Personal finance is personal. The method that you choose to incorporate into your Money Management System and the reason for making that choice will be different from others. I have personally tried debt consolidation, balance transfers, Debt Snowball, Debt Avalanche, and the Blizzard methods of debt repayment. I have attempted them individually as well as mixing and matching techniques to create a unique debt repayment system that worked for my family's situation. It's all about knowing your situation and making the best choice for you.

How do you choose a debt repayment method to incorporate into your overall Money Management System? Before choosing which one to use, answer these three questions first.

- Is the method you're using the most efficient form of paying off your debt at this current point in your life?

- Does it help you save time?
- Does it help you save money?

I'm going to share some stories with you about how we went about choosing our methods, in addition to how we discovered it was time to move onto the next method. Even though these three questions are important, you may find that your values outweigh saving time or saving money, and that's okay. If it feels like everyone around you is pushing you toward a particular method, know that what everyone else wants may not be exactly what you want or need. Make the choice that best fits your finances.

Let's spend some time walking through the different repayment methods to get a better sense of what they are and how they work.

Debt Consolidation: Think of debt consolidation as one of those extra-large Ziploc storage bags that you can vacuum the air out of to make it smaller. Debt consolidation works similarly in that it allows you to take all of your debts, such as credit cards, personal loans, and medical bills, and roll them into one loan. The purpose is to create one smaller consolidated payment with a lower interest rate. Debt consolidation is tempting in that it offers a reprieve from having to deal with multiple payments and multiple interest rates. However, for many, it could lead to more debt if they continue using the credit cards that created the initial debt.

Balance Transfer: A balance transfer is an act of moving your debt from one credit card to another. Someone utilizes this method to transfer a high-interest-rate debt to one that has a lower interest rate or to one that offers a zero-percent-interest promotion. While a balance transfer gives you the ability to pay off your debt with more suitable terms, it's important to remember that the clock starts ticking on the amount of time allotted as soon as the transfer is complete. If you do not pay off the balance during the promotional period, the interest rate can jump from 0% to a variable interest rate as high as 29.9%. Some companies may also add the amount of interest that would have accrued on the back end of your loan. There is also usually a transfer fee based on the amount of money being moved. Be sure to read the terms and conditions of the balance transfer before signing up.

Debt Snowball: The Debt Snowball Method is a popular debt repayment method centered around motivation. This method allows you to have small wins early, which is perfect for someone who is just getting started on their debt repayment journey. This method disregards interest rates. Instead, it focuses on the debt balance. When put into practice, you list the balance of all your debts from smallest to largest. Then, you start with the smallest debt. Once it is paid in full, the amount you were initially paying towards the first debt is then rolled into the next debt, thus making the amount you can pay larger. As you continue using this method to pay off your debts, you'll find that the amount you can pay towards the debt has become significantly larger in the same way you would imagine a snowball becoming bigger as it rolls downhill. A downside of the Debt Snowball is that it could end up adding more to your debt without you realizing it, especially if you have a more substantial debt with a high-interest rate that sits at the bottom of your list.

Debt Avalanche: This method attacks a major factor in debt accumulation, the accrued interest. Instead of worrying about how much debt you owe, your focus is on eliminating the debts with the highest interest rates first. The benefit of this method is that it cuts down on the amount of interest you would pay over the life of the debt because the balance is reduced at a faster pace than just paying the minimum balance. Although you may be saving money over time by using the Debt Avalanche, depending on the amount of your debts with the higher interest rates, you are less likely to experience the quick wins of the Debt Snowball.

Debt Blizzard: The Debt Blizzard is a combination of the Debt

Snowball and Debt Avalanche. Depending on your situation, you may start with the Debt Snowball to pay off smaller debts and free up excess cash, and then you switch your method to the Debt Avalanche so that you're able to clear debts with higher interest rates. The benefit of this method is that it allows you to experience both debt repayment strategies; however, you could experience early burnout or wind up adding more debt onto your overall balance due to accrued interest, depending on how you blend the two.

As my husband and I started our Broke on Purpose journey with a large amount of consumer debt, we wanted to choose a strategy specific to our situation. We choose to start with a popular strategy of the Debt Snowball. We knew that it would fit perfectly into our Money Management System and allow us to systemize our debt payoff. Like many people, we had to make a mindset shift to stick to a repayment strategy. Here we were, willingly choosing to put the bulk of our excess money towards debt instead of using it on ourselves. We were excited, we were motivated, but we were still a bit afraid of what this entire process would look like. I'd personally tried to pay down debt before and failed repeatedly. My Facebook memories occasionally remind me of these failings, showing me a post where I talked about how I was finally going to get out of debt, only to see again later that I never actually did it. Because I didn't want to fail again or revert to default behaviors, I knew experiencing small wins upfront would be important. That guided us to the Debt Snowball.

Below, you will find an example of what our timeline for paying off all our consumer debts would have looked like had we stuck with only making the minimum payments. If you're like me, you can't fathom making 176 payments for fourteen years to pay off items you probably don't have anymore.

REGULAR PAYMENT PLAN

	TOTAL AMOUNT DUE	MINIMUM PAYMENT	REMAINING* PAYMENTS
AMAZON	$90	$25	4
SUNGLASS HUT	$261	$25	11
BEST BUY	$409	$25	17
J.C. PENNEY	$1095	$68	16
PAYPAL	$1495	$25	60
UPROMISE	$4324	$80	54
CAR LOAN	$5307	$392	14
TOTAL	$12,981	$640	176

*NUMBERS ARE APPROXIMATE

The Power of $100!

It may not seem like it, but any amount you can throw at your chosen debt repayment method beyond the minimum payment is going to reduce the amount of time you spend paying a debt. Take our situation, for instance. If we only paid the minimum payment on our debts, it would have taken us approximately 176 payments over 176 months before everything was paid off. Keep in mind that this does not include the amount of interest we'd also have to pay. Now, look at what happens if we were to add an extra $100 each month to the minimum payment starting with the Sunglass Hut debt while using the Snowball Method. It would reduce the amount of time it took to pay off our debt from 176 months to approximately 15 months! If that is what $100 could do, imagine if you were able to add an extra $250 or even $500? The more you pay beyond the required minimum payment, the faster your snowball gains momentum.

To reduce the amount of time our income had to be funneled to our Debt Repayment Station and accelerate our debt payoff, we put the above principle into overdrive. By adding extra money from our part-time work

THE POWER OF $100!

and side hustles to the minimum payment each month, we were able to accelerate our debt repayment strategy and pay off $7K of our $12,981 consumer debt in just two months! Play around with your numbers to see how this particular debt repayment method could benefit you. Look at how much time you'd save if you added extra money to each payment versus following the minimum amount only way of debt repayment. Also, consider what's important to you in saving time or saving money and if that particular repayment method is the most efficient.

THE POWER OF $100

	TOTAL AMOUNT DUE	MINIMUM PAYMENT	NEW PAYMENT	REMAINING* PAYMENTS
AMAZON	$90	$25	$90	0
SUNGLASS HUT	$261	$125	$215	1
BEST BUY	$409	$125	$340	1
J.C. PENNEY	$1095	$168	$508	2
PAYPAL	$1495	$125	$633	2
UPROMISE	$4324	$180	$813	5
CAR LOAN	$5307	$492	$1305	4
TOTAL	$12,981			15

*NUMBERS ARE APPROXIMATE

Switching Debt Payoff Methods Can Save You Money!

Using the Debt Snowball, we were able to pay off over $41,000 of our debt (which included some student loans) in 13 months. However, just like any system, you're going to have to continually monitor the output and progress of the individual stations within your Money Management System to make sure that the current settings are efficiently producing the desired output. While the Debt Snowball Method proved to work very well, in reevaluating our debt payment plan, we realized that continuing with the Debt Snowball would surprisingly result in us acquiring more debt due to the size of our student loan balances combined with the interest rates.

Armed with this information, we had to take a step back and revisit those three important questions for choosing a debt repayment strategy. Our current method was no longer saving us time or money, even though it was the right strategy to use at first. Because of this, we knew we needed to adopt another method and make some significant changes to the process and procedures we currently had in place within our Debt Station.

As I mentioned previously, the Debt Avalanche is a method that

SWITCHING DEBT PAYOFF METHODS

focuses on eliminating your high-interest debts first. Instead of paying your debts off from smallest to largest, you are now paying them off in order of highest to the lowest interest rate. Having finished all of our smaller debts, my husband and I decided to aggressively tackle the student loans. There were three loans left with balances of around $41K, $51K, and $89K. Trust me. Every time I write these numbers, I cry a little inside. Of this, $21,893 was solely interest that accrued while the loans had been in deferment.

Here's an inportant detail you need to know considering student loans. You cannot begin to pay off the principal balance on your student loans until the interest has been paid off. The only problem with that is YOUR INTEREST ACCRUES DAILY! Depending on your payment plan, the minimum payment only goes to satisfy a portion of the accrued interest. As interest accrues daily, you are collecting more interest on top of the interest that has already accumulated. This is compounding, but with debt instead of investment earnings. It's a never-ending cycle, and the only way to get out of it is to make sure your minimum payment is enough to cover the accrued interest and a portion of the principal balance.

Our largest student loan had a balance of $89,000. $18,539 of that total was accrued interest (I just cried a little bit there, too). Since our interest charged at a rate of 6.8% accrued daily, approximately $13.58 was added to our balance every single day, totaling up to about $407 a month. In order to get caught up on this loan, it was important that we started paying it down before the deferment ended or that interest would be capitalized onto the backend of the loan.

When planning out which method to use in your Debt Repayment Station, it's important that you are aware of all of the numbers. To find out how much interest you're accruing daily on your unsubsidized, private, or subsidized student loans that only start accruing interest after graduation, you can use this formula:

START HERE

(Interest Rate)(Total Amount Owed)/365

By putting all our numbers into an Excel spreadsheet, we determined that in three years' time, if we continued using the Debt Snowball Method to pay off our debt, we would accrue an additional $15,706 on top of the $89,000 loan. Granted, we could have factored in salary increases and other income changes, but those things weren't guaranteed. The daily interest accrual however, was. If we instead switched to the Debt Avalanche Method, we would significantly reduce the amount of interest over the life of the loan. This, in turn, would save us a very large sum of money.

For this change in methods to work, we had to be strategic and look at the best way to use all the resources available to us to help achieve our financial goal. We discovered that using a combination of two debt repayment methods, the Debt Avalanche and a balance transfer to a credit card that offered a promotion of 0% for 18 months, was our best option for three reasons. First, it would allow us to start making minimum payments on the loan to reduce the principal balance. Second, it would reduce the amount of interest that accrues over the life of the loan. Finally, it would allow us to pay off the $18,000 of interest on our terms.

Before making the commitment to transfer the balance and put this plan in place, we had a money meeting. In this meeting, we weighed the pros and cons of this action. Sure, moving the $18K to a 0% interest vehicle would save us money, but we'd also be losing the protections and benefits that federal student loans offered. Because there was so much at stake with this decision, we committed ourselves to pay off the transfer in 6 months instead of the allotted 18 months.

To decide which debt repayment method will be the most beneficial for you to include within your Debt Station, use the list of debts you created and walk through the pros and cons of each method. Although

SWITCHING DEBT PAYOFF METHODS

we personally used three methods to help us pay down a majority of our debt, you may find that you only need one. The most important thing to keep in mind is that what works for someone else may not work for you. Just because everyone else is choosing to make payments a particular way doesn't mean you have to follow the crowd. There will be methods that are very tempting, like debt consolidation or doing a balance transfer; however, if you haven't mastered the habits that put you into debt, these methods can easily lead you back down that road, as they give up the false perception of your debt being paid off. In reality, the debt is just moved from one place to another. I've fallen into that trap before and wound up with double the debt and double the stress because I still hadn't learned how or why I was getting into debt in the first place.

When building your debt repayment system, use the method that feels most comfortable and only take on what you can reasonably handle. Also, rembmer to break your debt's size into mentally manageable pieces. Using this way of thnking will allow you to set monthly payoff goals that you can realitically achieve. To pay down $18,000 in six months, we had to work a lot of long hours and extra jobs, but we knew that the sacrifice was only for a short time. To us, the benefits outweighed all other drawbacks we came up with. The debt repayment methods that we incorporated into the Debt Station of our Money Management System went a long way toward helping us organize how we would pay off our debt. However, our ability to pay down debt quickly came from taking on extra jobs and by reducing expenses. Remember that the more money you can throw at your debt, the faster you can pay it off.

Not Everyone Wants to Be Debt Free and That's Okay!

Being debt-free is the new sexy; however, what often gets lost in that perception is the reality that being debt-free is not a primary life goal for everyone. Many simply want the breathing room that comes from reducing debt, as opposed to eliminating it entirely. This goal is just as admirable and celebration-worthy as saying you want to be debt-free. The great thing about your Money Management System is that it allows you to explore your options. You set the pace for how fast or slow you want to go and what your overall financial goals are. When we initially started living Broke on Purpose, being debt-free was the only thing we could wrap our minds around. The thought of no longer owing anyone was intoxicating! However, as the months turned into years, we slowly realized that while we'd dug ourselves out of over $100K of debt, we were also burned out from the constant grind of working full-time jobs and side hustles. After making a substantial end-of-the-month payment, I would find myself sitting on the couch in a daze. It looked like I was over the moon in my Instagram post, but in reality, I was trying to wrap my mind around doing it all over again the next month. Knowing it was a means to an end helped

NOT EVERYONE WANTS TO BE DEBT FREE

a little, but I still had to force myself to get over the mental and physical exhaustion and keep going. After three years of working to be debt-free, we knew we had to pivot.

A pivot can either be forced by a life situation, or it can be a strategic action that you implement on your own. If you're experiencing burnout or if things aren't working as well as you'd hoped, it might be time to pivot into a different direction. You can choose a route that will still align with your goals but take you on a different path to get there.

By making a few tweaks to the structure that we already put in place within our Money Management System, we could reduce the flow of our income into the Debt Station and reallocate more to the Non-Retirement and Retirement Savings Stations. The things that were important to us before were still important, but they were not as crucial. Because of this pivot, we allowed ourselves the freedom to focus on building wealth, creating memories, and living a life that we loved.

Thanks to the added influence from social media, there is an increased pressure to continue down paths that no longer align with your goals. There is a lot of talk about sacrifice, but does anyone know what that entails in the grand scheme of things? How much are you willing to miss out on to make an extra payment? Think about it: Grandma won't turn 94 years old again. There is no guaranteed next time. We're often told to push ourselves to the max when it comes to saving and paying down debt. What do you gain by living to such an extreme that you miss out on spending time with loved ones or miss out on laughing with friends? The older I become, the more fragile I realize life actually is. I believe that we should all live in a way that makes sense to us. One of the great things about being human is that we have the ability to multitask. Don't let your debt repayment plans cause you to forget what's truly important to you.

Create Your Debt Playoff Plan

As you continue to build your Money Management System and your Debt Station weigh the pros and cons of each debt repayment strategy and come up with a debt repayment plan that works best for you. Consider the importance of saving time, money, and how the strategy fits your current situation. With this plan in place, plug it into your Money Management System. To do this, add the debts to your B-SP, so that it can appropriately purpose the money. If you have a lot of debt, you may find that a large chunk of your income from your B-SP is being directed to your Debt Station. Because this is your personal Money Management System, you can go full throttle by pushing all the extra income flow into your Debt Station. You can also reduce your speed by realigning some of that income to fund more non-essential expenses or savings. If there isn't enough money to cover what needs to flow in your Debt Station, consider taking on extra jobs or looking for other ways to cut back. As you pay off each debt or meet your goals, the money that was once flowing into your Debt Station can be repurposed elsewhere.

It can be tempting to try and pay off your debt as fast as the next person but remember this is not a race. It's a journey. Journies don't start and end quickly; they go through dips and valleys, triumphs, and victories before reaching their endpoint. You may experience this while working on repaying your debt. No matter how stressful it may feel at times, don't quit. Keep going. It's okay to pause for a moment to restrategize, but don't let that pause turn into days, weeks, or months. Consistency is your friend here. For more detailed help, talk with a financial coach or counselor to help you develop a game plan that best fits your needs.

Manage Your Money Like a Personal Finance Expert

Learning how to manage your money isn't a one-and-done skill. While this book couldn't possibly cover every financial topic that you'll encounter, my goal is to give you the framework for building a Money Management System. This system will help you reduce the chaotic feeling of your finances, create organization and structure, incorporate seamless workflows, and allow you to spend more time doing the things you love. Admittedly, we covered a lot of ground here. With all great systems, work is done in the beginning, so that the rest of the journey is smoother sailing. When you take the time to build out your Money Management System, you are giving yourself a winning chance at meeting your financial goals. You're working smarter, not harder. With your Money Management System running smoothly in the background, it will look like you had a professional set up your finances for you. Little do others know, you don't have to be a personal finance expert to run your finances like one.

Not everyone has extra time to take a deep dive into every aspect of personal finance. Thankfully, not everyone needs to. With the framework for your Money Management System in place, you can manage your money effectively and meet your goals. Just remember these three steps:

STEP 1: BE NOSEY. Your Money Management System is a continuous loop from one station to the other. For the system to function properly, it is essential for you to know what information is being shared across stations, so that you can quickly catch errors. I'm not talking about getting glimpses here and there; I'm talking about being so nosey that Wendy Williams comes to you for the tea. You have to know all the details regarding the flow of income within your system. The easiest way to do that is to identify the WHO, WHAT, WHERE, WHEN, AND WHY.

Ask yourself these questions:

WHO are we paying? By knowing everyone you owe money to, you'll be less likely to miss a payment.

WHAT are we paying for? Have you ever looked at your bank statement and noticed a charge for a subscription service where you don't recall signing up? Keep track of what services you're paying for so that you can be on the lookout for unnecessary expenses.

WHERE does the payment need to be sent? Can we pay online, does it need to be dropped in the mail, or should it be hand-delivered to a specific location? By knowing where the payment needs to go and how the payment can be made, you can better plan for it. Make a note in your financial calendar or schedule the amount to be automatically sent from your bank on a specified date. You might even be able to schedule a payment using an online bill pay method.

WHEN is the payment due? Is there a grace period for making payments? Find out if you can make payments early without penalty. What is the late fee associated with missed or late payments? If you miss a payment, call and politely request removal of the late fee. It doesn't always work, but it is worth it to try.

WHY are we paying this amount? Bills fluctuate. If you receive a bill and the amount seems higher or lower than usual, do your due diligence

START HERE

to find out why. There is a chance a promotion may have expired, you received a credit, or something wasn't correctly calculated on your account. To share a personal story, when we received a higher-than-average electric bill one month, I discovered an article that talked about a rate hike from our power company. Armed with this information, I knew to plan out more in our B-SP Station in the upcoming months for our electric bill.

STEP 2: BE ANNOYING. How many telemarketers or robocalls have you dodged today? The reason why you get so many is that there is a high probability that if enough calls are made, someone will sign up for their offer or fall for their scam. When it comes to your finances, be persistent like those telemarketers. This persistence allows you to maintain an accurate Money Management System. If something doesn't make sense on your account or statement, call to get clarity!

While you may hate having to fight through pressing the right button or sitting on hold with that horrible music, you can get a lot more resolved by talking to an actual person. Ask questions until you get the answers you need. If you find the person on the phone isn't able to give you the information you need, politely ask to speak with someone who can. If you still are unable to find adequate answers to your question, hang up and call back again. As most calls are sent through a communications center, you're bound to be put in contact with someone who may know more than their colleagues.

STEP 3: BE A KNOW IT ALL. Just like most managers or supervisors, you're going to have to become the "know it all" when it comes to your Money Management System. You know that person in your group of friends who seem to have a "well, actually" response for everything someone says? That's going to have to be you with your finances. You're going to have to know the ins and outs of your system so well that you can tell if an employee is quoting their Terms of Service wrong when you call to ask about a bill. You're not becoming a "know it all" to show off;

you're doing it to protect yourself. If you don't know something is wrong, you can't expect companies to be honest and tell you that something is wrong.

To become the "know it all," you have to consume one piece of financial information every single day. I don't mean you have to get a degree or take certification classes, but you should make financial literacy a daily part of your life. Doing this is as easy as listening to financial podcasts, studying a few pages of a book (which you're doing now), reading a blog post, tuning into webinars, or even simply reading news articles in magazines like *Kiplinger's* or on sites like Money, Black Enterprise, or Businessweek.

The more financial information you consume, the more your wealth of knowledge grows, and the better your Money Management System runs. Why? Because now you have the power to make informed financial decisions.

Final Words

Do you know why those in-home subscription meal kits are so successful? It's not because the meals are some of the best food you've ever eaten; it's because they offer convenience. When I think about why I could never seem to get my finances in order, I realized that everything I tried sold me a plan, but it never sold me the benefits of the plan in a way that I could relate to. Sure, I wanted to pay off debt and save more money. But what I was really looking for was something that allowed me to do those things and offered convenience at the same time.

Convenience does more than just make things easier; it allows you to do more with less. I spent way too much time struggling with my finances before incorporating my Money Management System. I was trying to focus on each individual piece instead of looking at my finances as a whole. This system saved me and it can save you. Even though I couldn't go back and change those sleepless nights worrying over bills and expenses, I could change my future. My Money Management System did exactly that.

By putting a system in place, I created a new protocol for my finances. With my Money Management System in place, I could see how my habits

FINAL WORDS

and behaviors affected the movement of my income, causing backups and delays. I could see how my debts and poor spending habits were siphoning all my money into my Debt Station, thus starving my Savings Station. I needed to see where my money was going wrong so I could make it right.

I want you to get that same detailed picture of your finances. Money can be complicated, but your personal finances don't have to be. I hope you take these blueprints and start building your ultimate Money Management System. The life you desire is just on the other side of you choosing to no longer be Aimlessly Broke. Set your goals and put the system in place to help you reach them. Regardless of what you've told yourself in the past, you deserve this. You are worth this.

I want you to start here. Start right now. Start today. I'm not going to tell you that it's going to be easy, but I am going to tell you that it's going to be worth it.

As you begin to build out your Money Management System using the blueprints that I've given you, you're going to see the interconnectedness of your finances and how the output of one station relies on the input from another. Your B-SP can't function without your income. Your Living, Savings, and Debt Stations can't function without your B-SP.

Once you see the big picture, managing your money gets simpler. You'll begin to experience the added benefit of convenience that your system provides you. Expenses that used to keep you up at night will be covered thanks to your sinking funds. You'll no longer ask yourself, "Where did all my money go?" Instead, you can track every movement. You'll step into the role of Money Management Supervisor, and you'll understand how important your decisions are to your system's final output. Your Money Management System puts you back in control of your finances!

I know you can do this. You know you can do this! You'll achieve this by creating a healthy space in your life that allows you to be intentional with your money and focus on your financial goals. You'll reframe your

START HERE

mindset by moving from a place of scarcity to a place of abundance. You will have the ability to get 1% better each and every day. Don't mistake what you feel to be slow progress for inaction. Time and consistency are your friends. One dollar a day can grow to millions if you let it! Becoming debt-free doesn't have to be your goal. You may just want to create room in your finances that allows you to breathe. Either choice deserves applause. No matter how you design your Money Management System, know that through the successful management of your money, you'll have the power to create the life you want.

Notes

Dump The Defaults
1. Wendzich. R (2019) Default Settings: Adjust your Autopilot to Build a More Stable and Impactful Life. Rad Wendzich

Parental Persuasion
2. Lino, M. (2017, January 1). The Cost of Raising a Child. Retrieved from https://www.usda.gov/media/blog/2017/01/1/cost-raising-child
3. Guthrie, G. (2019, September 24). Americans think financial education classes should be mandatory, survey finds. Retrieved from https://www.consumeraffairs.com/news/americans-think-financial-education-classes-should-be-mandatory-survey-finds-092419.html
4. Horton, J. (2012, June 13). Study reveals who influences the financial behavior of children. Retrieved from https://www.moneymanagement.org/blog/2012/06/study-reveals-who-really-

influences-the-financial-behavior-of-children

5. Ages & stages of numeracy development. (2009). Retrieved from https://www.cccf-fcsge.ca/wp-content/uploads/RS_95-e.pdf
6. T. Rowe Price's 11th annual parents, kids & money survey. (2019, March 21). Retrieved from https://www.slideshare.net/TRowePrice/t-rowe-prices-11th-annual-parents-kids-money-survey
7. de Blasio, B., & Salas, L. (2018, November). Student loan debt distress across NYC neighborhoods: identify indicators of vulnerability . Retrieved from https://www1.nyc.gov/assets/dca/downloads/pdf/partners/Research-StudentLoanDebtDistressAcrossNYCNeighborhoods.pdf
8. Zapp, D. (2019, May). 2019 money matters on campus. Retrieved fromhttps://everfi.com/wp-content/uploads/2019/05/MoneyMatters-2019.pdf

Demystifing Your Net Worth

9. Bowden, J. (2019, May 31). Net worth of Americans aged 18 to 35 has dropped 34 percent since 1996: study. Retrieved from https://thehill.com/policy/finance/446372-net-worth-of-americans-aged-18-to-35-has-dropped-34-percent-since-1996-study

The Cost of Cohabitation

10. Orman, S. (2007). The money book for the young, fabulous & broke. New York, NY: Riverhead Books.

How To Have a Successful Money Meeting

11. Kogon, K., Blakemore, S., & Wood, J. (2015). Project management for the unofficial project manager. Dallas, TX: BenBella Books.

NOTES

How Much Money Should I Have in My Emergency Fund

12. McGrath, M. (2016, January 6). 63% Of Americans don't have enough savings to cover a $500 emergency. Retrieved from https://www.forbes.com/sites/maggiemcgrath/2016/01/06/63-of-americans-dont-have-enough-savings-to-cover-a-500-emergency/#35e9f7f34e0d
13. Timm, J. C. (2019, January 8). Government employees could go without pay for nearly a month, at least. Retrieved April 9, 2020, from https://www.nbcnews.com/politics/donald-trump/government-employees-could-go-without-pay-nearly-month-n955741

In It For The Long Haul

14. Dennison, S. (2019, September 23). 64% of Americans aren't prepared for retirement - and 48% don't care. Retrieved from https://www.gobankingrates.com/retirement/planning/why-americans-will-retire-broke/
15. Start saving up for retirement in your 20s. (2020, February 10). Retrieved April 9, 2020, from https://www.usaa.com/inet/wc/advice-retirement-savinginyour20s

Saving When You Don't Have Anything Left To Save

16. Martin, E. (2019, January 9). The government shutdown spotlights a bigger issue: 78% of US workers live paycheck to paycheck. Retrieved April 9, 2020, from https://www.cnbc.com/2019/01/09/shutdown-highlights-that-4-in-5-us-workers-live-paycheck-to-paycheck.html

Made in United States
North Haven, CT
14 June 2022